P9-CEU-850

Refresh
Renew
Revive

Refresh
Renew
Revive

H. B. London Jr., Editor

PUBLISHING

Colorado Springs, Colorado

Library of Congress Cataloging-in-Publication Data
Refresh, renew, revive / H. B. London Jr., general editor.
p. cm.
ISBN 1-56179-467-8
1. Clergy—Conduct of life. 2. Clergy—Religious life.
I. London, H. B.
BV4011.5.R46 1996
248.8'92—dc20 96-24695
CIP

Published by Focus on the Family Publishing, Colorado Springs, CO 80995. Distributed in the U.S.A. and Canada by Word Books, Dallas, Texas.

The chapter in this book by Eugene Peterson originally appeared as "The Good-for-Nothing Sabbath" in *Christianity Today*, 4/4/94. The chapter by Francis Schaeffer is taken from *The Complete Works of Francis A. Schaeffer* (Crossway Books, 2d ed. 1990), vol. 3, pp. 5-14. Both are used by permission.

People's names and certain details of the case studies in this book have been changed to protect the privacy of the individuals involved. However, the facts of what happened and the underlying principles have been conveyed as accurately as possible.

Editor: Larry K. Weeden
Front cover design: Candi L. Park
Front cover photo: J. P. Fruchet/FPG International

Printed in the United States of America

96 97 98 99/10 9 8 7 6 5 4 3 2 1

CONTENTS

Acknowledgments

As you look back over a project like this, you realize that many people played crucial parts and deserve to be thanked publicly. First, I'd like to express appreciation to Dr. James Dobson and the board of Focus on the Family for giving us the privilege of ministering to pastors, both in this book and through our ongoing outreach to them.

Next, my thanks go to all those who contributed either a chapter or a sidebar. Their honesty and insight, most of which was first given in the "Pastor to Pastor" tape interviews and has now been put in this written form, are what make this book a worthwhile investment of your time.

I also thank William E. Henry for doing such a fine job of taking those interview transcripts and converting them into the chapters you'll be reading here. A pastor himself, Bill shares our same heart for ministry, and it shows in these pages.

My secretary for 24 years now, Sue McFadden, was invaluable as usual, coordinating the project from our end, keeping me organized, and translating my handwritten scratches into my part of this book. Kelli Drury, another member of my staff, provided research for the project.

Jan Nations produces the "Pastor to Pastor" tape series with excellence, so she played a vital part in the original assembly of the material in these pages.

My thanks also to the Focus on the Family publishing team for pulling together all the pieces of this project. Al Janssen, Director of Book Publishing, encouraged me to do the book and made it all happen. Larry Weeden, Senior Editor, aided by Betsy Reinheimer, Editorial Assistant, led me through the whole publishing process with patience and grace, as well as doing the hands-on work of turning our mutual dream into a finished reality.

For all of us who have played a part in creating this book, it has been a labor of love. We hope that as you read it, pastor, you will sense our respect and concern for you and your family. And we pray that you will be encouraged and built up in your walk with the Lord and in your ministry. God bless you!

Introduction

by H. B. London Jr.

I have known nothing but a pastor's home. My dad was a district pastor in the state of Arkansas when I was born, and he served the greater church until he passed away in February 1996. My mother was the consummate pastor's wife and in many ways set the standard for her role. I'm an only child, as is Jim Dobson. As my first cousin, he is the closest thing I have to a brother. He, too, came from my same background and tradition. He tells the story of our heritage in both *Straight Talk to Men and Their Wives* and *When God Doesn't Make Sense*. I'll let him use his own words to fill in some of the details.

> How can I explain the prayers of my great-grandfather (on my mother's side), who died the year before I was born? This

wonderful man of God, G. W. McCluskey, took it upon himself to spend the hour between 11:00 A.M. and 12:00 noon every day in prayer specifically for the spiritual welfare of his family. He was talking to the Lord not only about those loved ones who were then alive. McCluskey was also praying for generations not yet born. This good man was talking to the Lord about me, even before I was conceived.

Toward the end of his life, my great-grandfather made a startling announcement. He said God had promised him that every member of four generations—both those living and those not yet born—would be believers. Well, I represent the fourth generation down from his own, and it has worked out more interestingly than even he might have assumed.

The McCluskeys had two girls, one of whom was my grandmother and the other, my great-aunt. Both grew up and married ministers in the denomination of their father and mother. Between these women, five girls and one boy were born. One of them was my mother. All five of the girls married ministers in the denomination of their grandfather, and the boy became one. That brought it down to my generation. My cousin H. B. London and I were the first to go through college, and we were roommates. In the beginning of our sophomore year, he announced that God was calling him to preach. And I can assure you, I began to get very nervous about the family tradition!

I never felt God was asking me to be a minister, so I went to graduate school and became a psychologist. And yet, I have spent my professional life speaking, teaching, and writing about the importance of my faith in Jesus Christ. At times as I sit on a platform waiting to address a church filled with Christians, I wonder if my great-grandfather isn't smiling at me from somewhere. His prayers have reached across four generations of time to influence what I am doing with my life today. (*When God Doesn't Make Sense*, pp. 202-3)

Now Jim and I have the privilege of working together at Focus on the Family. It was a decision that came after a great deal of prayer and conversation. We were both raised in a matriarchal environment where our moms insisted that the extended family gather frequently for special days and vacations. We had a wonderful time growing up in our various locations and church situations; and believe me, for both of us, some places were better than others. We learned very early the challenges of living in a pastor's home and the pressures of being a pastor's kid. In 1985, through God's providence, I became the Dobsons' pastor. It was during our time in Pasadena that we began to discuss the burden on clergy families. We talked openly about how much of the crisis mail received at Focus on the Family was out of the pastor's home.

One evening in the course of our conversation, we explored the possibility of our working together. The chance of that appeared pretty remote, but in subsequent times together, the subject would resurface, and one day we said, "If it's okay with Beverley and Shirley, and God doesn't stop us, let's give it a try." And we did. In November 1991, I resigned my pastorate in Southern California and moved immediately to Colorado Springs to begin my assignment as a pastor to pastors. It has been one of the most rewarding and challenging assignments of my professional life. I thank God for the opportunity.

Early in my tenure at Focus on the Family, Jim and I did a radio program. We outlined the ministry, shared some of our vision for this new endeavor, and talked about the joy of working together. The program received a lot of encouraging mail, but one letter I will never forget was from an 87-year-old female listener in her scrawling script. It was addressed to both of us — "Dear Dr. Dobson and H. B." She began by saying how great it was that the two of us could work together and share in a joined ministry. She went on to talk about other things, and then in the concluding portion of her letter, she said, "Oh Dr. Dobson and H. B., it is such a joy to know that the two of you will be spending your declining years together." And so we are.

The "Pastor to Pastor" tape series began in October 1992. We have completed 24 editions and have not begun to cover all the issues confronting pastors and their families. The response to the audio cassette format has been gratifying. One pastor's wife wrote us, "We are enjoying 'Pastor to Pastor.' The tapes are so insightful and full of encouragement for the journey. God bless your ministry to pastors." A leading pastor in the Northeast wrote us, "I can't tell you what it means to receive 'Pastor to Pastor.' Though in the ministry for over 30 years, I feel like it's going to be a pastor's forum each time I listen. Your leadership and choice of speakers is tops. Please tell Dr. Dobson how much that ministry is appreciated." And from one of the thousands of pastors who shepherd a smaller congregation, "These tapes help me keep up with new and different ideas, as well as challenge my thinking ability by working through these topics. 'Pastor to Pastor' fills a need as I am unable, due to distance, to form any close friendships with other pastors." And one more letter from a pastor who, like so many, listens to "Pastor to Pastor" in his automobile: "I began listening to the first volume and found myself anxious to drive somewhere so I could listen again. The information has been tremendously helpful to me as well as my wife."

We are both humbled and thankful to so many pastors and Christian leaders who have taken time to affirm our decision to begin "Pastor to Pastor" in the first place.

The format is relatively simple. We choose the subjects for discussion that come from pastors and their families through our mail and telephone calls. Then, with the help of our producer, Jan Nations, we select the guests we feel can best address the issue. Finally, we sit in a studio and talk. The engineers and editors make the necessary corrections on the recording. Mike Trout and I come in together and do the "wrap-arounds," the distribution center assembles and packages the product, and "Pastor to Pastor" becomes a reality. It has truly become a labor of love.

One day, our book editors came to me and said, "What would you think about turning the 'Pastor to Pastor' audio series into a book?" I jumped at the chance, because I know from what you tell us that it's almost impossible to assimilate all the information you hear from our experts. Now we have *Refresh, Renew, Revive*. A writer and pastor named William E. Henry, who lives in Sebring, Florida, has spent literally hundreds of hours taking the spoken words from the tapes and putting them into the written word. He has done a remarkable job.

We received permission from our chapter guests to reproduce their words in a book. Every one of them said they would be honored to be included. We are blessed by their participation. We added some classic writing from Francis Schaeffer and Eugene Peterson. The editors allowed me to put my spin at the beginning and end of each chapter. And now, after more than a year of work, our dream has become a reality.

The title and subtitle—*Refresh, Renew, Revive: How to encourage your spirit, strengthen your family, and invigorate your ministry*—in itself expresses our intent. We very much want you who read our book to experience all the above. But even more than that, we want you to know how genuinely loved and appreciated you are by Focus on the Family and all of us who had anything to do with this project.

You are of inestimable value and worth. You are called upon, like prophets of old, to take a stand and deliver a message that is increasingly unpopular. We realize that unless you have the opportunity from time to time to become refreshed, renewed, and revived, you will run the risk of spiritual burnout. We pray for you and want you to know we are available to you. We want to hold your arms up as Aaron did for Moses. Allow us to be your Jonathan, your John Mark, your Barnabas. We're on your side. Come on in and look around. We believe that as you turn the pages of this volume, you will be blessed by what you find.

~ 1 ~

"Weary and worn" is a phrase we often hear from pastors at Focus on the Family. I don't think our colleagues are complaining, I just think they're stressed to the "max" and need to find a place where they can lean back against a shade tree and relax.

One pastor wrote us recently, "I grow weary. . . . I wrestle with my own needs—how to continue fresh in spiritual growth, how to nurture family life, how to be faithful and accountable in my personal life." He probably could have continued with a longer list of things that help to create challenges in every aspect of his ministry. We all could. That's why we must do something about the pace we keep or we will be overrun.

I have found in my years of pastoral experience that our congregations not only have unrealistic expectations for us, but they also will let us serve ourselves into the ground if we choose to do so. Balance is a great word for every one of us. If we don't stay balanced in all aspects of our living, we wear out in one way or another. It won't be the same for any two of us, but out-of-balance pastors will one day suffer the consequences of their choices either spiritually, morally, physically, or relationally. In time, our ministry will rob us of our joy.

In this helpful chapter, Archibald Hart raises the caution and then helps us find the solution to the all-too-prevalent problem of stress and burnout in the clergy.

Arch Hart is a dear and valued friend. I admire his wisdom and can follow his logic. When I pastored in Southern California, he was a highly regarded trainer of ministers at Fuller Theological Seminary. I know one thing for sure: Archibald Hart loves pastors, and he wants to help them complete their course in a victorious manner.

H. B. London Jr.

Stress and Burnout

by Archibald Hart

A Case Study

Loren Sanford made a mistake that he would encourage every pastor to avoid: He began with a counseling ministry, and then he planted a church out of that ministry. Consequently, he says, there was an implied contract.

"The fact that I started the church out of a counseling office meant that what got written into the genetic code of the church was this expectation that I would be available to nurture all these hurting people one-on-one," Sanford says. "So my burnout began with trying to pastor what became a rapidly growing church at the same time that I was carrying an enormous counseling load."

Because he was doing so much of his work out of the counseling office, he wasn't drawing healthy people but rather people who had tremendous brokenness, which they carried into their relationships in the church. Eventually, they ended up fighting with each other.

The burden of trying to keep the church at peace, provide an incredibly exhausting counseling ministry, teach, and run the programs of the church was just too much. He began to run dry. "When people would come and ask me for ministry, I felt as if I was being tortured," Sanford says. "I'd go to get my resources, and they just weren't there."

He felt anger, because he was being used. And he felt God had betrayed him—had actually set him up for disappointment. "He would give me a promise and then deliver the opposite," Sanford says. "I also felt He wasn't defending me—I was being persecuted and lied about by people. I felt as if I'd been used by Him without any regard for my own needs." Eventually, he came to question God's love for him.

The Cause

Sanford's father was a pastor, so Sanford had seen how the demands of the pastorate had increased over the past 30 years. "What's happened today is that people are asking the church to be everything," he said. "We're looking at a time when families are disintegrating and fathers are absent from homes, and people are asking that the church fill all their needs. If they need significant psychological counseling, they want it from the church. If they have a family relational need, they want it met through the church. If they have significant dysfunctions in their lives, they want them dealt with through the church."

Clearly, that's far too big a demand for the pastor and his wife to fill, or even for the church as a group (usually) to fill. Yet many pastors try, working 10, 12, or more hours a day. But if (when) they can't meet people's expectations, disappointment and complaints are sure to follow. Then pastors, like Sanford, can end up feeling betrayed by God and betrayed by people. They keep serving God, but where is their joy in ministry?

How to Regain Control?

Can you identify with a lot of Loren Sanford's story? Pastors frequently find themselves physically exhausted and spiritually depleted. They are the casualties of a system of ministry that is insatiable. Something always needs to be done; new demands must be addressed; more people require special attention.

It may be that your heart was palpitating just yesterday, and maybe your head is throbbing even now. Maybe this is the fifth week you've gone without a day off, and every hour of your calendar is filled with critical meetings.

How do you regain control of a way of life gone haywire?

Adrenaline

Ministers in the Western world keep too hectic a pace. We're constantly on the go, and we live on adrenaline. In fact, you could say we're addicted to adrenaline. We like to begin new projects, to focus on new challenges, to take onto our shoulders new and different tasks. And it's the adrenaline that keeps us going. Especially on Sunday!

Caught up in this high-stress lifestyle, we live in denial. Remember, being hooked on adrenaline is an addiction to a high, to excitement, to challenges, to new projects. We don't like doing the old, routine stuff; we don't like maintenance. We like planning new ventures. And as in all addictions, denial is a factor.

Look at a good man like Bob Pierce. He started World Vision, and he burned himself out early in life. His daughter has described how he got into the difficulties that led to his death. She said he believed it was his obligation before God to give 100 percent of his effort 100 percent of the time. He was on the road 9 or 10 months of the year, and he felt that God was obligated to take care of his family at home while he was out solving the problems of the world.

The trap in what happened to Bob Pierce is that what he did looks almost biblical, doesn't it?

Yes, it looks almost biblical. But Satan is an extremely intelligent enemy, and if he can't take your foot off the accelerator, he will put it down very hard for you.

Every minister I know feels lousy on Monday. You see, the day of heavy adrenaline draw is typically the day of worship, when you have to perform (so to speak) and be in the pulpit and so on. When that adrenaline then comes down, you go into a discomforting depression.

Many ministers spiritualize this depression. They see it as a spiritual problem. "Satan's getting to me." But mostly it's bad adrenaline management—it's primarily the consequence of having used too much adrenaline, being too charged up, too revved up (biologically speaking), over the weekend.

Much of what we do in ministry does require a lot of adrenaline. Take preaching, for instance. If you're going to keep people awake and not put them to sleep, you've got to have some energy going. It's the overuse of that system of energy, though, that leads you suddenly to crash on a Monday morning and puts your body into what is known as a post-adrenaline depression.

What are the symptoms of that adrenaline letdown? You're irritable; you don't have a lot of patience; you want to be quiet; you don't want to talk; you don't want to see anybody. For scores of pastors, that's the gift they give their spouses on a Monday. And to make matters worse, that's the only time many of those wives get to be alone with their husbands! It's not quality time, and it's not adequate for building a good marriage. Wives say, "I get out of the house on Mondays. I split. I don't want to be around him."

That's why I suggest that pastors use Mondays to do some low-level, routine activity. Tidy your desk, throw out the trash, read some magazines, or sharpen those pencils you always want to sharpen when you're trying to work on a sermon! It should not be a period when you get your adrenaline going again. It's not the time to pick a fight! And it's not the time to hassle anybody or to let anybody hassle you, because if you get your adrenaline up again, you'll feel all right—but you will have robbed your body of its needed time for rest and recovery.

Monday, then, is not a good day to take off. Take a day later in the week—maybe a Thursday or a Friday—when your energy is good, you feel alive, and you can give your family some quality time.

This whole discussion leads us into thinking more deeply about two vitally important topics for pastors today: stress and burnout. Just what are they, and what can you do to defeat them—or at least manage them?

Stress

Stress and burnout are two different things. Let's look at stress first.

Stress is primarily a biological phenomenon. As I said, it comes on when you've used too much adrenaline, when you've been too much on a high. Stress produces a state of emergency in the body—the body is, in effect, in emergency mode. Cholesterol goes up, blood pressure rises, your heart beats faster, and your hands get colder. This accelerated wear and tear eats away at your stomach to produce ulcers, gives you high blood pressure, and even starts to clog your arteries and put you on the road toward heart disease.

Burnout

Burnout is more of an emotional response. In burnout, things are not going right. The resources aren't there. People are not affirming you, and a state of demoralization sets in. For me, the key concept in burnout is that one word *demoralization*. You no longer care.

Burnout occurs when you don't have adequate support—when you don't have someone with whom to talk and share your burdens.

Consequences

Both roads—stress and burnout—lead ultimately to depression.

The depression that comes from stress is due to the exhaustion of the adrenal system. On the other hand, the depression that comes from burnout is the loss of your vision, of your ideals. You become demoralized, and you don't care anymore.

A fellow from the Harvard Medical School identified the process leading to aberrant behavior in secular leaders. I see it at work in our Christian world as well. Specifically, the devil uses four A's to lead a minister into big trouble.

The first is *arrogance*. The minister says, "I can do it myself. I don't need anybody else's help." And then he begins to make the rules. He doesn't obey the rules—he makes them.

That leads, secondly, to a sort of adventurous *addiction*. The pastor becomes taken up with what he's doing, very excited and energized by it, and it's an addiction.

Then he begins the third A: *aloneness* sets in. That's the point at which depression is a risk, because he cuts himself off from other people.

And then, finally, there's the danger of *adultery*. The minister turns to sex as the only thing that will give him his kick, as a way to make up for what he has lost, because he has a profound sense of loss.

Those four A's are as much a risk for pastors as they are for anyone in the secular world who's striving to be successful. They are the consequences of too much stress.

Type A and Type B Personalities

The type A pastor would normally try to break down the doors to solve the problem of stress. But the risk for the type A personality is that after a while, you become so arrogant that you don't think anybody can assist you.

The type A pastor says, "I don't need any help. I can do it myself. I know that everybody else thinks we should do this project a different way, but after all, I make the rules here."

Now, *arrogance* is a strong word, but it describes the way many pastors come to feel. And left unchecked, that arrogance can lead through the other two A's to adultery.

The type B pastor, on the other hand, is much more often a victim of burnout rather than stress. Because type B people are more thoughtful, and loss for them is a much more painful thing, they're not as susceptible to the four A's. Being much more introverted, though, the type B pastor does not tell others about his pain. And that leads him to burnout.

The Solution

Besides taking a day off other than Monday, you can take four other steps to combat stress and burnout.

Step 1: Face up to your symptoms.

The first step in dealing with either stress or burnout is to face up to your symptoms.

If stress might be your problem, is your blood pressure up? Are you getting sick often? (Frequent illness is a sign that your immune system is being compromised, possibly by too much stress.) Are you having periodic depressions triggered by that adrenaline switchoff? Any of the classic stress symptoms that come regularly must be taken as a sign that you're pushing your system too fast and too hard.

On the burnout side, the signs are much more subtle. Slowly you find yourself beginning to hate the telephone. When it rings, you jump. You begin to avoid people. You may also find yourself becoming narrowly focused on petty issues. Let me illustrate.

I once knew a pastor who was in an advanced stage of burnout. His study was on the second floor of the church building, overlooking the parking lot, which was next to a supermarket. And he would sit in that study for hours, looking out to see if he could catch people parking in the church lot when they were going to the supermarket. When he did, he would run down the stairs—the burned-out person is irritable and gets angry easily—and say, "How dare you park here! This is the church parking lot!" All this on a weekday, when nobody else was using the lot! But that's how petty his focus became.

Another sign of burnout is paranoia. You become suspicious. "Everyone's out to get me." "People are talking behind my back." "What did they mean by that?" "What did he mean when he stood up in that committee meeting and said such and such?"

These are all signs that you're losing your perspective and balance. You need to face up to these symptoms.

Step 2: Learn to rest in Christ, our Sabbath rest.

The second step in dealing with stress and burnout is to learn to rest in Jesus Christ, our Sabbath rest. The Bible speaks of this in Hebrews 4:1-11. Often, though, our evangelical world is even more adrenaline-dependent than the rest of the world. We're committed to fulfilling the Great Commission, and, obviously, that means work. But somehow, in all that, we've lost sight of the importance of being able to rest in Christ. We must learn not to usurp His work—only to be a servant to it.

Remember that God wants us to use our time wisely. We need to learn to say no to some things so we can say yes to the things God really wants us to do. He will equip His people for the accomplishment of the Great Commission. And He gives different people different gifts. Seek His face in prayer to learn what He wants you to say yes to.

And remember what I said about Satan: He's an extremely intelligent enemy, and if he can't take your foot off the accelerator, he will put it down hard for you. Don't let him do that.

Step 3: Take care of unfinished business.

The third step in dealing with stress and burnout is to take care of unfinished business.

Of the books I've written, the one that I did most for myself is *Adrenalin and Stress*. My wife says I wrote that book because she prayed for me. It chronicled my battle with stress. I needed to deal with it, because I had a lot of unfinished business from my childhood that I had carried into adulthood.

I would encourage you to really think seriously about what unfinished business there may be in your life as well. Some pastors, for example, have had a bad experience in one church and then move on to the next church and the church after that, and they've never dealt with the letdown—the disappointment—in that earlier experience.

Whatever it is for you, resolve—in the strength the Lord gives—to deal with the unfinished business in your life.

Step 4: Seek peer support.

The fourth step in handling stress and burnout is to seek peer support.

Burnout comes when you don't have adequate support—when you don't have someone with whom to talk and share your burdens. To return to Loren Sanford's case, listen to what he said on this matter: "If you're on the road to burnout, you're living in a world that's going to become more and more insane if you're alone in it. So I strongly encourage you, if you're on that road, to find another couple who are not in burnout (whether they are laypeople or another pastoral couple). You need to meet regularly with them, and you need to make a discipline of saying, 'This is what I'm feeling. Pray for me.' Just share things. When you confess your sins to one another (as James 5:16 says), it has the quality of objectifying what's inside you and therefore making it more livable. You make things not insane anymore."

Sanford continued, "These need to be people who aren't going to give a lot of unasked-for advice. They need to be people who aren't going to tell you that sin is the cause of what you're in, because you're already broken and you don't need a bunch of Job's comforters."

This is important, because whether it's a stress problem or a burnout problem, we have to resist overloading the family system for the solution. It's wonderful to have an understanding wife. But don't depend solely on her for the emotional and spiritual support and healing you need.

I hear scores of pastors' wives saying, "He dumps on me. I dread the moment he comes home and opens that door, because I know what's going to happen. He doesn't want to listen to my problems. He doesn't want to hear how the kids have been acting up. He thinks that's all petty stuff. And I have to sit there and receive all that dumping. That's not fair!"

So it's absolutely essential to build an adequate support system, preferably with peers to whom you can turn to share your heart and, in bearing one another's burdens, to find the healing Christ can bring.

According to surveys done by the Fuller Institute of Church Growth, 70 percent of pastors have no one they consider to be a close friend. And 50 percent have considered leaving the ministry within the last three months. If you're standing at the crossroads in your ministry because of stress or burnout, I would encourage you to look back at God's original call on your life to pastoral ministry and begin to rest in His sufficiency for yourself, for the health of your family, and for your congregation.

It's impossible for you to meet the needs of every member of your church. But you can be faithful to God's call nonetheless—to the truth He has revealed to you and to the discipline of balancing the priorities in your life.

I urge you to find one person this week with whom you can share the burdens of your heart—a friend, a prayer partner, someone who will encourage you, pray with and for you, and faithfully walk beside you as you lead others into the light of God's truth. Let me tell you about one way to do this.

Way up in Bangor, Maine, a group of evangelical ministers set aside time every other week just to get together. They meet for breakfast at a local restaurant so they can talk. There's no agenda. Sometimes the talk is theological; sometimes it's personal, such as when one of the group is having problems at his church. For these pastors, their meetings can be church, in a sense.

In Maine, you see, the trees outnumber the people by at least a million to one. It can get pretty lonely up there. But those pastors give one another the kind of support that can be a lifesaver for a minister experiencing stress or burnout.

Take the time for such mutual uplifting. If there's not such a group in your area, consider starting one. But find at least one person outside your family who can stand with you. You're too busy not to.

Pastor *to* Pastor

Stress and burnout. You relate—right? Are you truly facing up to your symptoms? Are you relaxing in Christ, your Sabbath rest? Are you taking care of any unfinished business in your life? And are you currently meeting with a group of your peers?

The preceding paragraph sounds like the outline to a four-point sermon, doesn't it? Just as you would want your people to think about a three- or four- point sermon you just preached—but more than that, you want them to act on the teaching of that sermon—just so, my fellow pastor, few things would please me more than to learn that as a result of this chapter, you began meeting with a group of your peers. I know how easy it is to put off that first step, but let me encourage you to take it. Even the Lord Jesus didn't minister alone, and the servant is not greater than his Master. Take the initiative and call a colleague before the day is finished.

Don't let this sound like a guilt trip. Don't let it be another burden on your overloaded shoulders. But I need—and want—to encourage you to take action in this very important area. I don't want to see your name on the casualty list! Rather, perhaps when we meet at a conference somewhere down the road, or through a note you scribble out and mail to me six months from now, you can share with me the good news of what this chapter has meant to you!

Hang in there, my friend! The Lord of the universe is rooting for you, and so am I.

H. B. L.

~ 2 ~

I'll never forget the day I completed the "Pastor to Pastor" interview with Gordon and Gail MacDonald that you'll visit in just a moment. The telephone conversation was over, and the studio engineers were busy finishing their work—but I couldn't move. I sat in the darkened studio with tears streaming down my face as I thought of so many of my brothers and sisters in ministry who had experienced brokenness. For a lot of them, that period of testing was the greatest lesson they could ever learn. But for others, it signaled the end of their pastoral journey, and shattered dreams were everywhere.

I recall a pastor who wrote me, saying, "I had been in the preaching ministry for 12 years until my forced resignation. The last few months have been very difficult for me and my family. My heart longs to be back in the ministry. The church I served had grown from less than 200 to nearly 1,000 in worship, but change was too much for the leaders, and things fell apart."

Did you catch that last phrase—"things fell apart"? That's brokenness. When things fall apart, we can feel life is so broken that even God can't fix it—but you know He can, and He will! The prophet Jeremiah learned a lesson of God's great love and power while watching a potter spin a wheel—he can make the vessel over again. He can rebuild the broken when it seems unmendable. So, too, we know that in God's hands, all things are fixable—even brokenness.

I first came to know Gordon MacDonald through his book Ordering Your Private World, *but I grew to love him and his wife, Gail, as I sat in a pastors' and wives' conference sponsored by Focus on the Family and listened as they not only confessed and agonized over their own brokenness, but also gave powerful testimony to God's healing presence. Read carefully these next few pages. They are filled with amazing grace.*

H. B. London Jr.

Restoring Your Soul

by Gordon and Gail MacDonald

How many times has your world been broken, either by yourself, someone you love, your church, or some situation?

Whether your broken world is a result of exhaustion, immorality, fiscal mismanagement, immaturity, or the irresponsible choices of others, this chapter is meant to help you discover the path to restoration. We want to tell you, from personal experience, about the restoration process and the power of God's grace uniquely available through the Christian community.

What Is a Broken-World Experience?

When we talk about "broken worlds," we mean anything that shatters your hopes and dreams or disrupts your family or marriage. Brokenness is anything that has a catastrophic result that could threaten your way of life, your ministry, or your relationships. No one is exempt from the possibility of suffering a broken-world experience.

Warning Signals

At least four warning signals can help you detect the approach of a broken-world experience. They are:

1. Not listening to criticism from your wife, church elders, and others

The first warning signal is when a person places himself above criticism and won't hear rebuke or the opinions or counsel of others, beginning first with his wife and then with close friends and colleagues.

Let's face it, when you become the head of an organization or a church (even a small or medium-sized church), you then have a group of people following you, and you have to become strong-willed. You build up a hard callus on your soul and on your mind. Now, that can be helpful. We all need to have thick skin at times, and stomachs that don't develop ulcers.

But the down side is that you can stop letting people get through to you when they're trying to talk with you about the state of your soul or the qualities they see in you that are eroding your spiritual and moral condition. You don't listen to the people—elders, deacons, church members wise and not so wise—who have the responsibility to say no to you sometimes. After all, you're paid to be right, aren't you? You're the pastor, and people expect you to be right. So you begin to breathe in the error.

I've stood at the door of a sanctuary and had a hundred or more people come out and tell me the sermon I just preached was the greatest thing they've ever heard. You know how much we pastors enjoy hearing those kinds of compliments. Then you go home, and your spouse—or even one of your children—wants to criticize some dimension of your life. Who are you going to listen to?

The result is that you begin to believe the favorable press notices. You flow toward where you're going to get strokes rather than toward the reality of what might be helpful. You don't listen to the people who want to truly assist you.

2. The traveling lifestyle

A second warning signal that a broken-world experience is a danger is what we call the traveling lifestyle. We travel a lot, so we know this danger firsthand.

One of the great restraints of sin is a fixed community in which people know you well and you're all committed to the same norms and behavioral standards day by day. At the risk of sounding simplistic, I (Gordon) go back to my childhood for a good example of this. In the first few years of my life, I lived in a very stable neighborhood where I was known to everyone as Don and Esther's boy, and all the shopkeepers knew I was the preacher's kid. You didn't dare misbehave in that community, because if you even smart-alecked anybody, your parents would hear about it within a couple of hours. And the neighbors took upon themselves the responsibility of correcting you.

But when you start living the life of many Americans today—where this day you're in Chicago and the next you're in San Francisco and the third you're in New York—who knows what you're doing from hour to hour? No one. What's more, no one cares. So there's a great danger in the traveling lifestyle. Think how much easier it is to leaf through a copy of *Playboy* at an out-of-town airport than it is in your neighborhood bookstore.

But this lifestyle isn't merely a literal and vocational matter. It dovetails with the rootless mobility of so many Americans. We can easily move to a part of the country where no one knows us—or cares what we do. Moreover, as America becomes less and less a small-town and agrarian society, the anonymity of urban (and suburban) life allows us to adopt the traveling lifestyle even if we never leave home. We're getting to the point where that neighborhood bookstore might as well be a distant airport terminal.

3. Success

Success is a third warning sign that a broken-world experience is a potential danger. When you feel that you're indestructible (in the sense of "I've got the world by the tail!"), you begin to own the ministry rather than manage it. You start to run on natural energy. ("Hey! Look what I'm doing so well! I didn't pray—and didn't seem to need it.") It becomes a process that will lead to your destruction.

Success quickly lifts you out of the realities of where the average human being is living. You begin to think of yourself as unable to be touched by all the things that do in other people. You're convinced you're immune to sin and failure; nothing's ever going to go wrong.

The danger of success isn't there only for the pastor of the megachurch, either. It's just as real for the big fish in the little pond—and for the little fish in the little pond. Even in a small church, you can get the idea that everything you touch turns to gold if the Sunday school grows, visitors show up at the worship service, you write something for the local newspaper, someone asks for a tape of your sermon, or you're recognized out in the community. The danger of success exists for us all.

4. Taking yourself too seriously

At times, some of us simply take ourselves too seriously, and we overrate our importance to the overall picture. This also can lead to a broken-world experience.

I was raised to take myself too seriously. From the earliest days of infancy, both in the church and in my family, I was brainwashed with the notion that somehow a destiny was riding on my shoulders that I'd better not botch. I think I'm not alone in that.

H. B. London Jr.

Many men—even pastors—are caught up in the sewage called pornography. But we don't admit it.

The thought life can hold us captive longer than anything else. The thought life, you see, is who we really are—where we really live.

In his book *Running the Red Lights,* Charles Mylander talks about struggling with lust in his own thought life. After trying, to no avail, to clean up his thoughts, he saw a film one day with the words, "Lord Jesus, protect me by Your blood." Chuck wrote,

"In a flash of insight, I knew that Christ's power was as near to me as that quick prayer. The inner voice of the Holy Spirit came with convicting and convincing force, and the Holy Spirit said to me, 'Chuck, it's time for you to shape up your thought life. If you don't, I'm through with you. I'm simply not going to use you for my purposes anymore. You'll go through all the motions; you'll also stay busy and remain in the ministry; but when everything is said and done, nothing will remain

There's a problem in our evangelical system of raising expectations so high that we lead each other to take ourselves too seriously. We come to believe that the changing of the whole world depends on our efforts. It sounds almost stupid to say that, but more than a few men and women out there are thinking that way right now. They're heads of organizations and heads of churches, and they go to work every day believing that all of history hinges on what they're going to do. If you ask these people, they'll deny it; but that's what they're thinking. When you start taking yourself so seriously—and not remembering Who is sovereign and Whose will will be done (with us or without us)—you're setting yourself up for something bad.

The Steps in Healing a Broken World

Some of us have already experienced a broken world—maybe more than once. Some of us, we're sorry to say, will still experience a broken world in spite of knowing the warning signs. What, then, are the steps for restoring your broken world?

1. Take seriously the biblical concept of repentance

The first thing you must do to come out of a broken-world experience is to take seriously the biblical concept of repentance. You must come to a moment when you realize that down

that really counts.'"

Think about the impact of that. Chuck then went on to say, "Most of us would rather die on the spot than live a useless life and stand before the judgment seat of Christ empty-handed, rottenness on the inside and nothing on the outside."

Finally, he added this simple prayer: "Lord Jesus, protect me by Your blood." It came often to his thoughts and lips. God honored it, and the power of temptation was broken.

This is not a cure-all. But it is surely empowering to say with real conviction, when tempted by a lustful thought or a desire for pornography, "Lord Jesus, protect me by Your blood."

deep in the innermost depths of a person is a foul, stinking mess of a thing called evil that defies rational description. It is just waiting there to ambush the mind, twist truth, and lead you into a broken-world experience.

You don't enter into repentance just for a particular act, either. That's where the popularized evangelical gospel has been too weak. What you repent of is a condition, which is a far deeper issue than repenting of a single instance of sin. We're not talking about someone's having committed sins number eight and nine, while someone else has committed sins number two and three; we're talking about the fact that we all share a common condition that is potentially destructive—and we mean viciously destructive. (That's why every person stands on level ground before God and before the cross.) So you repent not once, but you have to keep going back every day and recognizing with a fresh brokenness that the same evil that betrayed you years ago (maybe in another way) could betray you again tomorrow. It's there, and it's just as destructive as always.

The lifestyle of being a repentant person leads you to live with a constant awareness of God's grace and mercy. It prevents you from criticizing others. It keeps you on an even keel with your spouse, and it makes all the difference in how your wife relates to you.

Being a repentant person, in fact, ought to be a value that you put into your marriage from the outset. It's the idea of deciding to keep short accounts with each other, of learning to say you're sorry to heaven and to your spouse. Otherwise, your broken-world experience will be much different. If mercy hasn't been lived as a daily pattern in the offending spouse, then when the broken world comes, the innocent spouse can find it nearly impossible to act mercifully. But if your spouse has shown you mercy many times, and then a broken-world experience occurs, the pattern of repentance and mercy is in effect, and mercy can be extended.

Even at that, however, giving mercy does not come easily. It's a struggle. Enormous amounts of mercy are necessary when a broken-world experience occurs, and it doesn't come with the simple flick of a finger.

In the experience, you learn what it's like to live with deep pain. But in that pain is a purifying, and there's also a presence and a tenderness of

God's hand that we're not sure you can discover in many other ways. It's a paradox to say that, but our marriage is a prime example. It has been purchased at a much greater price than most marriages, and it abides now in a constant flow of grace and mercy that makes me (Gordon) love my wife more than ever before.

2. Receive forgiveness and grace from God and those around you

You cannot give yourself grace, you can't restore yourself, and you can't (ultimately) forgive yourself. They have to be given as gifts—first from God, and then from significant people in your life. God and the men and women who surround you say (to use a medical term), "We're going to be your splint." That's what restoration, accountability, and key relationships are all about when someone has failed.

The average pastor doesn't have close relationships. He has no one he would call a best friend. And that's a real danger. Many of us were taught in seminary that the pastor can't have close friends, that friendships are a sacrifice you make in the ministry. We're convinced today that that's a terrible thing to teach young men.

We have misunderstood the Bible's teaching. There is, in fact, a great sacramental value in the community of friendships, and the pastor who doesn't take prime time in his calendar for the development of friendships is setting himself up for failure. He can't afford to put solely on the back of his wife the responsibility for rebuking him and affirming him. And I (Gordon) am afraid I didn't know that earlier. I look back and realize that close friendships were a great missing link in my own view of spirituality.

In the last few years, though, we have deliberately set out to acquire a community of close friends. And we put those people and times together in our calendar weeks and months in advance. The problem with most pastors is that they keep saying to would-be friends, "We've got to get together sometime." But there's always a funeral, a wedding, an emergency, or an extra sermon to be prepared. So an hour before you're supposed to get together with your friend, you're canceling the appointment. When we realize that keeping those appointments is a sacred issue, we're going to get much more serious about these relationships.

Receiving forgiveness and grace from those around you also means that the person who's in the broken world has to listen to the elders of the church. And again, it helps greatly if the person has been practicing this throughout his life up to the time of the broken-world experience. We've seen a lot of people who find it difficult to let themselves be disciplined—to accept the principle someone is trying to communicate when he says, "You must not do this." But the discipline is essential to the healing.

The first indication that you're with somebody who doesn't understand this idea of receiving discipline is when he calls you and says, "I've just gone through a terrible experience! I've failed miserably! Now, just what do I have to do, and how long do you think it will be, before I can start preaching again?" When someone asks a question like that in the first few minutes of your conversation, you realize he's trying to skip over the first eight or so steps of healing, and he's really not interested in getting his soul scoured and finding out what went wrong. He's much more interested in "How quickly can I get through the pain and get on with life and business as usual?"

You have to have accountability people in whose hands you can put yourself and say, "I'm going to allow you to be the healing mechanism. You're going to call the shots right now, and I'm going to submit to you totally."

3. *Confess your sins to one another*

Often we somehow feel we're immune to the consequences of past sins or past rebellions, so we just repress them, and they become secrets. We know God knows about them, but we act as though He doesn't. Then we keep those things from people who are significant to us, and we have our own little worlds in which we live. We deal with the past in whatever way we've chosen, and then (in many cases) the past pops up when we least expect it. How can we deal with this issue of secrets in our lives?

First, we have to reexamine our theology. Those of us in the Reformation churches have fallen into the trap of believing that when we sin, it's an issue between God and us alone. Therefore, if we confess it to Him—and how many of us have quoted 1 John 1:9 a million times?—everything is okay.

We've missed the vital biblical concept of confessing our sins to one another—not all our sins, and not all the time, but sometimes. And the minute we take upon ourselves the responsibility to be our own confessor, we have set in motion the possibility of keeping secrets. The instant we sin, though, we resign our control over the consequences, and we can never know when those consequences will become visible and create a catastrophe. It may be that years later, that sin will catch up with us.

Again we see the value of community. In community, we can become open and transparent and not keep secrets, because those people will hear our confession of sin and weakness with grace. Once it's out and the sin is named, the consequences become severely diminished, because they've been washed first in the grace of Christ and then in the grace of the community.

4. Make any necessary lifestyle changes

As part of the process of dealing with a broken-world experience, you need to go back and do a careful inventory of all the environmental issues that could have allowed the deceit to take place. We've become very respectful of the issue of fatigue, for instance.

In her book *Keep Climbing*, Gail wrote a lot about disillusionment. And I (Gordon) found that for a number of years, I had been packing down my own feelings because I spent all my time tapping the feelings of others. Things like that have to be changed.

Gail and I also realized we didn't play enough. There was too much work and not enough time for diversion. But we need to be away from work regularly; we need laughter and friendship. And we have to be proactive about finding time for play; it's not something that just happens. It's something to plan.

What if You're Trapped in Brokenness Now?

A broken-world experience can destroy a marriage. Many of you reading this are going through such an episode right now. You're saying, "My spouse and I have no hope, no chance of healing. We may stay together because it's what we have and there's no other choice. But . . ."

What can we say to those of you who feel trapped in brokenness? What's your hope?

Follow, first, the four steps we discussed above. And then be prepared to take two more:

5. Keep in mind the power of the gospel

Know that your hope is in the power of the gospel of Jesus Christ. If the gospel can't heal the worst of situations when people are yielded, repentant, and open to discipline, restorative love, and the grace of God, then it isn't worth much. But we all know the gospel is worth everything, because God paid to make it powerful through His Son's death and resurrection.

6. Be part of a church that's committed to healing

We need to go beyond steps 1 through 5 and say that people who have broken-world experiences can have all the intention in the world to seek healing, but a lot of that is not going to work if the community around them isn't equally committed to healing.

One of the real tragedies going on all across the world where men and women, laity and clergy, have failed is this: They're in churches that have no will to bring about healthy healing.

When the church commits itself to being a restorative ministry, however, and men and women stop acting in sinful self-righteousness and start saying with tenderness, "We are committed to getting every broken player back onto the field again to serve in the kingdom, and no one is beyond restoration"—then we believe we're going to see a true revival break out.

The world can duplicate almost everything the church can do—except show grace. Neither the devil nor people who are being led by evil can replicate grace.

The church has been given the great privilege of restoring and releasing people. Jesus said He was going to give us the keys to the kingdom, and that's where they all are. So when the church becomes known as a place where gossip, criticism, and slander are nonexistent, and where the most broken person can crawl up the aisle, sob his heart out in repentance, and know a community of people will gather around him and say, "Life is new now! We're committed to your restoration!"—then we're going to see the church across the world experience a revival such as it has never known.

Probably the greatest renewal movement that could happen would be for the church really to learn how to restore others to grace. If the church can forgive, it will become a safe place where people will want to be.

Pastor *to* Pastor

This has been a sobering, serious chapter. But I'm glad for it. We need times of laughter, but we also need to read a chapter like this every so often and readjust our lives if circumstances call for it.

In 1995, a colleague—a brother in Christ—took his life in Clayton, Missouri. Timothy Brewer, pastor of the 3,000-member Central Presbyterian Church, was only 36, with a wife and 3 children. He had lost a portion of his leg when a train hit him earlier that year and had been back in the pulpit for just 4 months when he left a farewell note for his congregation. He wrote:

> *God forgive me for not being any stronger than I am.*
>
> *Since the accident, it seems that I've been fighting a losing battle with depression and despair. I feel like a drowning man, trying frantically to lift my head to take just one more breath.*
>
> *Out of the countless sins that I have committed in this life, it is my own wretched weakness for which I am most ashamed.*

Friends described Brewer as a perfectionist. One of his associates said, "Here was a man who set a very high standard for himself and, for one reason or another, felt he couldn't meet it."

Second-guessing in such a sober matter certainly borders on irreverence. But I can't help wondering if Timothy Brewer's life might have gone better if he had had some men—his elders, some colleagues, friends, or even just one man—with whom he could bare his soul and from whom he could find help. God so frequently chooses to help us through other people. Did Timothy have those other people? Did he have either formal or informal accountability? Did he have congregational support? Maybe he had one or more of those, but if he didn't, it could have made a tremendous difference.

To bring it home, my friend, do you have a group of men—your church board, vestry, deacons, or elders—with whom you can really tell it like it is? Is there an informal group that meets this need in your life? Is there a mentor—an older, wiser Christian—in your life who can help you keep your broken-world experiences from overwhelming you completely? Can you say, "It is well with my soul"?

H. B. L.

~ 3 ~

My wife, Beverley, jokingly accuses me of having attention-deficit disorder. She may be right. You would think that in time I would learn to slow down, but alas, I guess it will never be.

As I look back over the period God allowed me as a pastor, it seems that my life was one of constant motion. Always on the go—doing good things, but probably not always the best things. Like what? Like sitting quietly in the presence of God more regularly and allowing Him to have His say. I'm sure I could have saved myself some troubling moments had I listened more and acted less. And somehow I don't think I'm alone in those feelings. There are a lot of you type A's out there who can relate exactly to the things I'm feeling.

One bit of counsel I received early in my ministry was simply stated: "The number-one thing you owe your congregation when you stand before them on Sunday morning is a knowledge of your personal relationship with God." That doesn't appear to be very profound at first reading, but the more you consider the thought, the more you realize its validity. In those quiet, confessional moments with my Lord, He would be allowed entree into my soul and would speak openly with me about our relationship. Even under the guise of business and "pastor things," we have no good reason to absent ourselves from a regular private time with Him. Be honest with yourself now—how much time do you spend with the Lord each day, just talking and listening?

To stand before our people with dirty hands and an impure heart is to do a great disservice to them—and to the God we represent. We need never be guilty of that, however, because like a loving Father, He waits for us to crawl into His lap and just spend time.

Jerry Bridges has always been a hero to me. I don't know him well personally, but his book The Pursuit of Holiness *changed my life. He loves pastors and works diligently to help people like you and me draw closer to our precious Lord. You will learn from his words. Please read them carefully.*

H. B. London Jr.

Maintaining a Heart Yielded to God

by Jerry Bridges

Intimacy with Christ nourishes ministry. The pursuit of holiness keeps the soul in shape.

But what about your life and your ministry, pastor? When a minister feels perplexed, strained, or fearful, his life tends to become shallow, and his ministry becomes perfunctory.

Here is an excerpt from a letter that was sent to Focus on the Family by a pastor. See if it sounds like a pastor you know—or maybe like yourself:

> My greatest challenge is not to become so involved in the administration, visitation, and other tasks of the work of the Lord that I fail to spend quality time knowing the Lord of the work.

While many ministry frustrations are external and environmental—even out of our control—our only sure way to revitalize the church is to renew and maintain our own walk with God.

But how do you maintain your walk with the Lord when the day-in and day-out demands of being a shepherd and preparing sermons seem to consume all your time and energy? What do you do when you're unmotivated and distracted? Where do you turn when you sense a growing distance between yourself and God? How can you maintain a heart yielded to God? What can you do to recover the wonder of the gospel ministry?

The Need for Godliness and Discipline

I believe ministry flows out of our lives—out of who we really are. Therefore, we can't adequately convey spiritual reality to others if we're not pursuing holiness. Our congregations always pick up on our weakness and follow us into spiritual shallowness if we're not pursuing a holy character and a pure lifestyle.

Would your people describe you as "successful"? Would they describe you with the adjective *godly*? If so, that doesn't mean you are pastor of the largest church in the country. It means you're a spiritually authentic man who causes others to believe you live close to God. You see, the pursuit of holiness is amazingly attractive to the people we lead. And as pastors, we can be both holy and effective. We don't have to choose between the two. In fact, I would say that no pastor is truly effective who is not holy.

When pastors are on a "successful" fast track, receiving accolades and commendations from parishioners and peers, they can become less holy than at any other time. In seasons of "success," pastors sometimes try to paddle their own canoe. There can be too much pride, too much dependence on self, and not enough trust in God's transforming and sustaining grace. But that's an awfully human effort—paddling a canoe rather than moving ahead in the power of Christ. Hundreds of pastors are like that, though; they try to do ministry in their own strength without relying on God's power and grace. It's a subtle but deadly temptation to us all.

Think about this, though: What difference does it make if I had a great crowd and a big offering last Sunday if I find that my heart is empty so that I'm not satisfied with God and fulfilled in Him?

Success or lack thereof is never a reliable way to measure personal holiness. One true way to gauge your ministry, in this respect, is to ask yourself, *If the Holy Spirit were to back out of this effort, would it collapse?* Many ministries would continue because they are humanly produced programs. It's easy to forget that visible success is not the issue, but rather having a genuine relationship with Christ and absolute dependence on Him.

At the same time, there's a great need for our pastors to be men of discipline.

Chuck Swindoll's advice to young pastors concerning sermon preparation is this: "Be sure you have made it a major priority to become a faithful expositor of the truth. Then when the demands and the pressures of pastoral life begin to bear down upon you, you can hold yourself to your priorities."

It takes work to produce a good expository sermon. And so Swindoll concludes, "It's a matter of discipline really, isn't it? Put your tail in that chair and get that light on and get that pencil moving as you study the passage you'll be preaching on."

Swindoll is right: Good expository preaching is a matter of discipline. And so is maintaining a heart yielded to God. There's a lot of talk in America today about values. Joseph Sobran wrote somewhere that we need less talk about values and more about virtues. Certainly one of the virtues that needs to be revived is discipline—especially self-discipline.

If you're like many people, breaking established behavior patterns, whether they're related to sermon preparation, family relationships, or the devotional life, takes great effort. But I continue to find that the fresher my relationship with Christ, the more willing I am to yield to His prompting. That's the kind of heart I want to model for those I serve: a heart that's authentically pursuing the things of God so that when I stand in the pulpit, meet with a man I'm discipling, or do anything else, I stand as one who has wrestled with the truth I'm teaching. I want my heart to be right with God. And that takes discipline and a desire for godliness.

One big step you can take toward discipline is to ask the Lord—for as long as it takes—to *give* you discipline. Self-control is part of the fruit of the Holy Spirit mentioned in Galatians 5:22-23; so ask the Lord for it.

What else can you do? Don't despair. There are some practical steps you can take to maintain a heart yielded to God.

Four Practical Pointers for Maintaining a Heart Yielded to God

It can be hard for pastors to keep their hearts right with God. Seventy percent of the clergy who write to Focus on the Family don't have a close friend or confidant. They find themselves isolated and feeling responsible for large numbers of people, but since there's no one in whom they can confide, they feel they're the Lone Ranger. And at times they feel almost angry with God for putting them in the position they're in. Maybe you find yourself among this group. Discipline is part of the answer to this problem.

First, though, I would hope that all pastors could confide in their wives. I realize that isn't always the case. Some wives don't support their husbands' being in the ministry. Others of us, frankly, need to admit that we need to work on our marriages; then we'll be able to

Charles Swindoll

Pastor, let me encourage you to make becoming a faithful expositor of the Word a major priority in your life. That may sound trite to you, but it is a commitment that immediately goes to the block as soon as the demand, the pressures, the other priorities begin to bear down on you.

Determine that when it comes to the actual delivery of a sermon, you will refuse to shoot from the hip. And part of that is refusing to start late.

It's a matter of discipline, really, isn't it? It's a matter of thinking, *Sunday is coming very soon—quicker than I will feel comfortable!*

I set myself goals to reach a certain place by Tuesday, knowing that Sunday is coming. I have to have an outline in hand before I can really think through a passage. And to have an outline, I have to have read enough to put some meat on that skeleton. And to read in such a thoughtful way, I have to write some things down. So I'm getting into it by Tuesday.

I have to have a fairly-well-thought-through message by Wednesday evening, confide in our wives. But we have to be open with them—we have to tell them where we are spiritually.

I don't mean we have to open the door of our hearts and show every evil thought we've had. That would be going too far. But our wives can read us like a book anyway, so we need to be open with them and have them as our confidantes.

Second, we pastors need to spend an hour a day with the Lord—just for our own lives, to feed our own souls.

The first half of that time is for reading the Bible with a view to its ministering to "me." It's a time for listening to the Holy Spirit—for saying, "Lord, what do You have to say to me today?" Just read and make self-application for the first half hour.

The second half hour is for praying. Try not to pray about yourself during this time. Pray about the church, the nation, the assault on the family—things like that.

Let me illustrate from my own assignment. I worked in an administrative capacity with the Navigators, where I dealt with business and legal issues. But I was just as dependent on the Holy Spirit to enable me to function in this work as a pastor is in preaching or building a church. In my time alone with God, I kept reminding myself of my dependence on Him.

God honors such dependence. Every morning in my quiet time, I read the Bible and pray, but I would also take time to evaluate

because we have a newsletter that goes out to our congregation, and it has to be in print and mailed. That's a discipline for me—to have that in my secretary's hands, with material thought through enough to have given it a title, to know where I'm going, and what idea it is that I want to get across. And in the midst of it all, I have to be sure that my heart has been right so that I glean what it is that God is saying, not what I wanted to say.

Part of the Saturday-night panic of an unprepared pastor ought to be his guilt for being unprepared. I have to use the word *unfaithful*.

People will come to you on Sunday morning wanting to be fed, and you will be coming to that moment with a deep sense of guilt. And you should feel that way. That's the right kind of guilt. The Holy Spirit is saying, "You have not prepared for this moment."

I remember a mentor of mine saying that he worked for an older fellow—an old German pastor—who used to come to the pulpit, years ago, when he wasn't prepared. He'd try to prepare during the song service, and he'd say, "Lord, give me something to say. Give me Your message." And another song would be sung, and he'd say, "Lord, give me Your message." He said, "One day the Lord gave me His message. He said, 'Ralph, you're lazy. You're lazy. That's My message.'" And I think, without calling it any other name, it is pastoral laziness. Sloth is one of the major battles you fight as a pastor. You have to make your sermon preparation a priority.

My schedule is probably not much different from that of any other pastor living with the pressures of the pastorate. But I do struggle to maintain that time with the Lord. I have to say no to most other things in order to get that time with Him. It's absolutely vital.

I have to make my time with God a part of my time in the Word. I can't have two hours set aside for devotions and prayer and then another two and a half hours set aside for study for sermon preparation. I have to make my time of sermon preparation my time with the Lord.

whether I was depending on the Holy Spirit or on my own talents and the fine staff around me.

We need to put ourselves up against the gospel every day. By this frequent and intentional application of its truth, we build a continual realization of God's grace and its transforming effect on our character. We need to review every day whether we're living in that power and grace. And when we do such a daily reassessment, we get excited about the gospel at work in us and become so aware of the grace of God that we want to live an effective life—and it continually transforms us.

Pastor, your personal holiness is your first responsibility both to your church and to yourself, no matter how many hours you work or what pressures you experience. Your personal holiness is your first obligation, and also the extraordinary source of spiritual vitality.

Think of highly visible pastors and Christian leaders whose lives are filled to the brim. How do they travel, speak, write, administer a church, and still allow adequate time for the Lord to do for them and to them what we've just been discussing? Though the details differ in every ministry, the pressures to bypass daily renewing are real for every pastor regardless of the size of his church. Many pastors would say, "My life is out of balance. I don't have time to pray. I don't have time for my family. I don't have time to fulfill the expectations of my church. I'm going crazy."

All that adds up to the strong possibility that they're probably not spending much time with the Lord, either. Personal time with God is usually the first thing that goes in our busyness.

Some pastors work 60, 70, 80, or 90 hours a week and serve a congregation that's clamoring for still more attention. Few people realize that an effective pastor creates an increased demand for his time, so that he's at it early in the morning and late at night. And often he doesn't have time to fit God into his days.

But the truth is that he doesn't have time *not* to fit God into his equation. It's as essential as food and water and oxygen for him to be spiritually well; it's also essential for his congregation. All his success is going to come tumbling down, either in this life or at the Judgment, if he doesn't build personal holiness into his ministry. When we stand before God to account for what we've done, all ministry without Him is going to be sounding brass and tinkling cymbals.

We cannot build holy character into our people if we don't have it in our own lives. There's no way to give our people the spiritual realities of God unless we possess them ourselves. The real "resourcing" for ministry is personal holiness.

Third, ask God to keep you on a short leash, to give you a tender conscience. If I begin to stray in my thought life, or if I begin

Sometimes I'll just close my Bible, turn the light off, and say, "Lord, I cannot seem to work this through. I cannot seem to find out what You're saying. Please meet with me here. Talk to me about this. Help me get a breakthrough on it." He doesn't always do it at that moment, although I've had that happen. But I'm often chagrined, realizing that I was out too late last night, or that I'm burned out. I need my day off. I rarely go out or entertain at home on a Saturday night. When I go to bed on a Saturday night, I want to be able to turn the reel on in my mind's eye and unfold that message. If I can't, then I'm back up again in my study. I want to be prepared.

So you have to tell yourself the truth. If you're faking it in your sermon preparation, you're faking it. Most people know it, whether you're admitting it or not. Second, sit down with your calendar. Except for life-or-death situations, have your secretary cover for you. If you have to get away to do your study at home, take your books and go. You don't need a big staff to do that. Train your secretary to cover for you, and your people will learn to appreciate a pastor who takes time for study. They'll see the results.

Once you've told yourself the truth and gotten alone to study, it's still amazing how you can fiddle around—wiping dust off your books, getting a drink of water, going to the bathroom. You start reading an article in *Time* and—boom!—you catch yourself! Don't let yourself do that! Stay in the study. Put your tail in that chair, get that light on, and get that pencil moving. Start putting something on the page. Force the beginning of it. (I've forced it many times.) Tell the Lord you have to get this down. It's Thursday; you don't have many more days. Ask Him to give you the thoughts. When He does, you'll be thrilled with how it begins to fall together.

to rationalize about sin, I want God to stop me short and keep me close to Himself.

Maybe you've noticed how extravagant some Christian leaders become when their church is paying the bills—the kind of restaurants they patronize compared to what they do when it comes out of their own pockets. It's slippery business, and it's easy to dupe ourselves.

Let's say I'm a pastor, I do some traveling to conferences or denominational business meetings, and my church provides me with an expense account. Like any businessman, I'll face the temptation to fudge on that account. We don't intend to be dishonest, but we rationalize. We say, *Oh well, because I'm away from home, I deserve this*, or something like that.

Well, the truth is that we don't deserve something if it's wrong. But it's so easy to rationalize! I ask God to give me a tender conscience, because as Song of Solomon 2:15 says, "The little foxes . . . ruin the vineyards," and I believe the battle is won or lost in the little things.

We can take ourselves out of God's arena. We can find ourselves living in our own little world, doing our own thing, and then suddenly push comes to shove, and (because we lack the discipline) we aren't strong enough to resist. The power of God isn't working in us, because we took ourselves out of His arena. So we need the discipline to stay close to God. If we let little things go, the big things will devour us—maybe even wreck our witness and destroy our relationship with God.

Fourth, Jesus taught us in the Lord's Prayer, "Lead us not into temptation," which I think means, "Deliver us from temptation." So we should pray every day, "Lord, keep me from temptation. Keep me from the assaults of Satan. Keep me from being blindsided."

No matter how many hours a week you have to work, no matter what the pressures on your life are, your personal holiness and spiritual authenticity are your responsibility.

Taking Responsibility for Your Personal Holiness: Two More Practical Steps

But does this sound frustrating to you? Do you feel like the overbooked, overworked pastor I quoted at the beginning of this chapter? I've already touched above on the discipline you need, but let me mention two other things that will help. You can take action on both right now, and they will also assist you in the long run.

First, you need a reminder that it's the Lord's work you're doing, not your own. In my case, I have a pen with a pedestal holder on my desk, and I have taped to that holder a slip of paper with just a reference on it—John 15:5. "Apart from me you can do nothing," that verse says. So every time I look across my desk at that pedestal, every time I go to use that pen, I see John 15:5.

Of course, it can get to the place where you see it but you don't see it, and we all have to be careful about that. So change the reference periodically. Maybe you could assign one of your church members to put an appropriate reference there each Sunday! Another useful Scripture is the well-known story in Luke 10, where Martha was distracted over her business while Mary was sitting at the feet of Jesus. On that occasion, Jesus said to Martha, "Only one thing is needed" (v. 42). One thing! As an overworked pastor, I might tape that phrase—"One thing"—or "Luke 10:42" to the dashboard of my car or on the pedestal of my desk pen. Yet another good verse is Psalm 27:4: "One thing I ask of the LORD, this is what I seek: that I may dwell in the house of the LORD all the days of my life, to gaze upon the beauty of the LORD and to seek him in his temple."

Second, go to your board, whether it's the elder board, the deacon board, or the church council, and say, "Look, my highest and greatest responsibility is my walk with God. I've got to give that priority. And I have only X number of hours in the day. I require five hours of sleep (or eight hours—whatever your physical constitution demands), and I need to spend at least an hour a day in maintaining my walk with God. I need X amount of time with my wife and family. I need X amount of time for exercise. Now, I would like you to help me set my priorities."

Then say, "What, then, is the first priority?"

They may say, "Well, the preparation of your Sunday morning sermon." Or they may say, "Discipling six men." Whatever they say, that's number one.

Then you go to number two. Pretty soon you're going to run out of time in your day, but you've got six other things that you've been doing! Then the board agrees that those can't be done. And they agree that those things don't get done or that someone else in the church will have to do them.

That is taking responsibility for your personal holiness.

Pastors often mistakenly underestimate the layperson's understanding of spiritual realities. Any spiritually alert lay leader wants his pastor to be a disciple of Jesus who is growing in Christlikeness. Trust your lay leaders with the fact that you want to pursue personal holiness. In most instances, they will be supportive or even generous in helping you find ways to do it. And the discussion creates a commitment to follow through on your part.

Being an Example

Let's look at another letter written by a pastor. This one says, "My greatest challenge is to set a consistent Christlike example—first before my wife and children, then before my congregation. I truly long to be a spiritual leader and not the manager or CEO of a nonprofit organization—or merely to be a weekly Bible teacher—but to be someone who by virtue of his intimate relationship with Christ greatly influences others to be like Him as well."

That pastor has a worthy goal. And his goal is attainable, to a degree. First Timothy 4:12 says, "Set an example for the believers in speech, in life, in love, in faith and in purity." My suggestion, though, to him and to every pastor, is that you be honest with your flock about your weaknesses and failures. You see, the person who believes he has to set an example can fall into the trap of thinking, *They can't see any of my weaknesses or I won't be an example*. No, let them see the example of how a Christian acts when he makes a mistake, how a Christian deals with his weakness, and so on. You can be an example that way as well as by the virtues and discipline you do maintain by the grace of God.

I've been a Christian for more than 40 years, and the pastors who ministered most effectively to me sometimes came to the pulpit and said, "Hey, folks, I don't have anything to say today." That might surprise you—especially after reading about "Ralph" in the Swindoll sidebar—because coming to the pulpit without a sermon is a pastor's nightmare. But the goal of the pastor-parishioner pilgrimage is to pursue holiness together.

I remember one Sunday our pastor said, "I was ready to come to church this morning, and my wife wasn't ready. I got upset with her because she was going to make me late." By telling us that incident from the pulpit, he helped us see that he was one of us and that we must pursue holiness together. Let me add that this pastor was a godly man, and he didn't tell us every time something went wrong in his life, but by being open on occasions, he came across as a person who is eager to be like Christ. He conveyed both spiritual eagerness and day-by-day realities.

To an extent, a pastor has to be transparent. It really is preaching confessionally when a pastor is willing to stand before his people and say, "My feet of clay sure showed this week. Let me tell you how I . . ."

Transparency and confession—those words describe liberating acts for pastors and for the believers under their care.

Of Utmost Importance: Your Personal Walk with God

This leads me to "the bottom line," and that is your personal walk with God. If you want to be the best you can as a Christian husband, father, and pastor, it all centers on your personal walk with God—on *being* rather than on *doing*.

My favorite Bible character isn't David, Paul, or Isaiah, but Enoch. Genesis 5:21-24 tells us twice that Enoch "walked with God." Hebrews 11:5 says that Enoch "pleased God." We need to keep those two things in mind. To me, "I want to walk with God" denotes my relationship, my fellowship, with God. And that occurs not just in the hour a day I mentioned. That hour is the foundation, but all day long, I'm to be walking with God.

And then "pleasing God" speaks of my obedience, the outworking of holiness in my life. That's why Enoch is my favorite character. I think that if I keep those two things before me—to walk with God and to please Him—that's all He asks me to do.

> With what shall I come before the LORD
> and bow down before the exalted God?
> Shall I come before him with burnt offerings,
> with calves a year old?
> Will the LORD be pleased with thousands of rams,
> with ten thousand rivers of oil?
> Shall I offer my firstborn for my transgression,
> the fruit of my body for the sin of my soul?
> He has showed you, O man, what is good.
> And what does the LORD require of you?
> To act justly and to love mercy
> and to walk humbly with your God. (Micah 6:6-8)

There will always be a tension, a struggle, between the gritty discipline of spending time with God and the great joy of loving to spend time in His presence, in devotions and in walking with Him. There will always be that conflict because every Christian is, as Luther said, at the same time both justified and a sinner. Walk with God and please God. Be and do. Work on the discipline, and ask God to provide the joy, for it, like self-control, is a part of the fruit of the Spirit.

Do You Need a Spiritual Vacation?

Allow me to quote from one more letter written by a pastor and received by Focus on the Family. It says, "The burdens of ministry are so great! I'm preacher, counselor, secretary, and sometimes maintenance man at our small church. I carry a heavy burden for the spiritual, physical, and emotional well-being of my flock. Satan is always attacking in one way or another. Sometimes I don't have the energy to fight the battle anymore."

What advice would you give that pastor? Or does he sound like you?

Frankly, I think that pastor needs a vacation. But I don't mean a vacation for taking his family on a tour of a theme park. He needs a vacation to get away and repair and strengthen his relationship with the Lord.

If a pastor is in the situation this letter described, for him it's just as it is when a person is physically ill. He has to back off from things. If a person goes in for major surgery, he's out for six weeks. That's just the way it is. The doctor says, "No, you can't go back to work." And if a pastor has reached the point this dear brother described, there's a spiritual illness, and it's going to take some time. It's not going to be repaired merely by the hour a day that I've emphasized.

That hour a day is maintenance for a healthy pastor. The pastor who wrote this letter won't get well by simply continuing his normal work. He's on an endless treadmill. He needs to take his "fiscal" weekly Lord's Day (other than Sunday—which is a work day for pastors). He needs to talk with the church's governing board about his schedule and about a sabbatical. And his board needs to give him a spiritual vacation.

Recovering the Wonder

All of us who minister need to recover the wonder of being a forgiven sinner. Along with that, we need to recover the wonder of getting to speak, in our day-to-day life and in the pulpit, for God.

I think it was D. L. Moody who, when he was quite old, was asked, "How do you keep going? How do you keep preaching?" And he said, "I never lost the wonder."

Whether you're ambitious to be a great pastor or in need of a spiritual vacation to regain the wonder (or both!), let this story from H. A. Ironside warm your heart to spend time with God.

Ironside told of a godly man by the name of Andrew Fraser who went to Southern California to recover from a serious illness. Though this old Irishman was quite weak, he opened his worn Bible and began expounding the truth of God's Word in a way that Ironside had never heard before. So moved by Fraser's words was Ironside that his curiosity drove him to ask the man, "Where did you learn these things? Did you learn them in some college or seminary?"

The sickly man said, "My dear young man, I learned these things on my knees on the mud floor of a little sod cottage in the north of Ireland. There with my open Bible before me, I used to kneel for hours at a time and ask the Spirit of God to reveal Christ to my soul and to open the Word in my heart. He taught me more on my knees on that mud floor than I ever could have learned in all the seminaries or colleges in the world."

If you want to be a great preacher of God's truth, spend a great amount of time with the Author of that truth—both in daily Bible reading and prayer, and in walking with God throughout the day.

Pastor *to* Pastor

I was impressed with the events that surrounded Cal Ripken Jr.'s record-setting performance of 2,131 consecutive baseball games played. What he said made a great point with me: "I just go out every day to do the best I can."

When he didn't feel like playing, when the team was losing (21 straight at one time), when attendance was down, when he had struggles at home or was in a batting slump—he still put on the uniform, headed for his position at shortstop, and gave it his best. Cal Ripken will be remembered as one of the greats of baseball as much for the character he demonstrated as for the incredible record it allowed him to set.

In ministry, longevity is a greater tribute than recognition. A willingness to bloom where God has planted you, to give it your best every day to His glory, is all He asks. What the people in the pew are saying is less significant than how God grades your faithfulness. Stay close to Him . . . at least one hour every day.

I'm seeing a lot of my colleagues failing to go the distance, giving up or caving in. But we are instructed, "Let us not become weary in doing good, for at the proper time we will reap a harvest if we do not give up." I'm rooting for you!

H. B. L.

4

Beverley and I celebrated our thirty-ninth wedding anniversary in August 1996. We were married at a young age and spent 31 of those 39 years in pastoral ministry. The other 8 years were given to ministry preparation and now at Focus on the Family. If we had to point to one thing we might have resented in our pastoral experience, it would be the limited amount of time we had for ourselves. Like so many of you, we lived in a glass home, where the light was always on and the phone was always ringing. If we didn't carve out time for ourselves, ministry responsibilities would rob it from us.

The problem of quality time together in the clergy household seems to be prevalent. All our surveys at Focus on the Family, as well as studies by a national magazine committed to helping ministers, find that lack of quality time together is the number-one problem ministry couples face.

One pastor's wife wrote me, "I understand the feelings of being lonely. Where do I fit in as a pastor's wife?" Another expressed, "I yearn for sweet fellowship with my pastor/husband—devotions and prayer time together. But it all so often gets crowded out by time pressures."

Can't you hear the anguish in those two honest notes? The truth is, according to a 1995 Hartford Seminary study of pastors from all denominational and independent groups, the incidence of divorce among clergy couples was the same percentage as that of laymen—around 23 percent each year. Our marriages are at risk!

In many of the talks Beverley and I would have on the time issue, she would bring an abrupt end to the discussions with "You know you can do just about anything you really want to do—and that includes spending time with the boys and me." She was right. The one key lesson all of us need to learn is the art of balancing our schedules in such a way that valued time is given to those most precious to us. As John Trent will tell you, "It's all a matter of priority."

John Trent is the kind of man all of us would want for a brother. He's intelligent, articulate, gifted—but most of all, he's fun to be around. You always feel better when you've been with him. His schedule is about as full as that of any man I know, but as you'll see, his life is also protected by parameters. Please take note, pastor. If John can do it, so can you!

H. B. London Jr.

Taking Care of Your Marriage

by John Trent

Marriages are under great stress and strain in America today. Far too many fail. This is as true for pastors and their wives as it is for lay couples. But to the sources of strain that nearly every marriage faces today, add the unique strains on pastoral marriages, and you can see why some—most?—pastoral marriages are in trouble.

Perhaps your marriage is troubled. If I were to arrive unexpected at your house today, would I see lines on your and your wife's faces that would indicate all is not well between you? Could I tell from your body language or the way you communicate (or don't communicate) that you're making yourselves do church business, but your marriage is in trouble?

If we were to sit down and talk honestly about the state of your marriage, would you say, "John, our marriage is in disarray. We're going through tough times. We're trying to keep up an image. We can't afford not to be in ministry. Can you give us some help to get us on the road to recovery?"

And even if you're doing well with your spouse, we can all use encouragement to keep our marriage sound and growing.

Let's look at some ways to strengthen your marriage, or to get it back on track if that's what you need. But first let's identify several stresses and strains on you and your wife.

High-Risk Relationships

Scripture talks about the need for you to be an example to the people in your congregation. It says, "Set an example for the believers in speech, in life, in love, in faith and in purity of heart" (1 Tim. 4:12). It also says, "In everything set them [the young men] an example by doing what is good" (Titus 2:7). "Be shepherds of God's flock, . . . being examples to the flock" (1 Pet. 5:2-3). Paul wrote, "Join with others in following my example" (Phil. 3:17). Elsewhere he said, "Therefore I urge you to imitate me" (1 Cor. 4:16) and "Follow my example, as I follow the example of Christ" (1 Cor. 11:1).

All these verses are true. But the heavy weight of living them out can become an unbearable demand for many pastors. Instead of letting our people see how a Christian lives out marriage in a fallen world, we think we have to show them a perfect life and a perfect marriage. According to a survey, an incredible 94 percent of all pastors feel their home needs to be the perfect home!

So what do we do? We put up a front that says our homes are in great shape. We—and our wives—know this isn't the way it's supposed to be. It's a terrible stress. But let me ask you: How many times have you gone into the pulpit knowing things are not right between you and your wife? How many times have you actually preached on things—giving others advice—when those very things were amiss in your own marriage? Most of us know all too well the expectation of perfection for the pastor's family—and the hypocrisy it can produce. We can reach the point where we think things in our marriage are hopeless and simply can't be turned around. And Satan is winning a victory.

People also expect the pastor's children to be perfect, and, let's face it, they expect you and your ministry to be perfect. The expectation may not be as great as it was in the past, but there's still a tremendous and subtle sense of high demands. And that leads to extra stress.

What's worse, with these triple expectations often comes half the support. I call this the "Everyone Else Is Close to Them" syndrome. The typical parishioner looks at the pastor and his wife and thinks, *Ah! They're obviously too busy to go out to lunch. All that church work! They're too busy to get close to. And besides, they must have tons of friends. I see other people talking to them all the time—they're probably worn out from talking with people!*

Well, we may be worn out from talking to people, but we're not worn out from friendships. Studies show that the average pastor and his wife are incredibly isolated. So in the face of all those expectations, there's only half the support (if that) for which we might hope. Stress and more stress, but too few friends to talk with about it all!

Pastoral work often provides only half the financial resources that other kinds of work can provide, too, which adds still more stress to the picture.

Let's face it: Being a pastor puts you in a high-risk category.

Men and Success

Before we go on to some solutions, though, let me set the stage a bit more. Let's talk about men and success, especially pastors and success.

What are men rewarded for, even as little boys? We're rewarded for being successful. And what is success? We learn this early as kids: We have to work like crazy, and then we make the football team. Then we work even harder to try to make first string. We're rewarded for all our hard work.

The problem is that the average pastor has labored long and hard to go to graduate school and learn Greek and Hebrew, and he spends time and takes great care studying the Scriptures, and he puts in countless hours at the church. But he learns, at one point or another, that he won't be

Karen Mains

My husband thinks that being the spiritual head of his home means that he will answer one day concerning whether his wife and his children developed their full potential before God.

So one of the things that I know David would ask you, pastor, is this: "Is your wife developing to her full potential?" When you look your Lord in the face, I trust He will say to you, "Yes, you did a great job as a pastor." But what will you say to Him if Christ says to you, "Did you free your wife—did you enable her—to do the things I also had in mind for her to do?"

I think this is a wonderful idea for you as a pastor, and for all husbands, to think about and talk over with your wife.

rewarded in terms of money the same way he might be in a lot of secular jobs. And that's one of the primary ways grown men measure success.

Being success-driven, though, we strive for ministry rewards—growth and numbers (and sometimes money)—as signs of success. And what often happens is that as we're working hour after hour for some recognition of all our effort, we absolutely zero out any time for intimacy in a relationship with our wives.

The very thing that many of us as men have used to define ourselves—which is success through hard work—is the very thing that robs us of intimacy. So we put up a front, having just the image of a good marriage, as I said earlier.

Often, one person in the marriage will want to do something about the situation. He or she recognizes there's a problem in the relationship. But the other partner is afraid of "word getting out that we're in trouble" and wants to let things slide and get by as they are.

When one person shuts down in a relationship, the heart reason is often emotional anger that has gotten trapped inside. For example, in the case of a pastoral couple that I worked with, the wife said to me, "Let me tell you what my husband's priorities are. They are ministry, ministry, ministry, ministry. Then family, and then ministry." Then she added, "I'm sick of it, and I'm out of here."

Over the years, frustrations had built up, and anger had gotten into her life.

What we often don't realize is that we're so wrapped up in trying to be successful and help everyone else (the people-pleasing and all the expectations of pastoral ministry) that the closest person to us can be the person we offend the most.

Why? Because we figure, *Oh, she'll cut me the most slack. There are only so many hours in a day, and I've got to please all these other people, so my wife should just assume she's the one who can be cut out. After all, she's committed to me! I have to cut somewhere. I have to be able to relax and be myself somewhere. I can't work everywhere!*

That's when the wife can pull back. But when she does, a lot of anger builds up, and that's when you see her put up a wall. Once the anger reaches the breaking point, she explodes like the wife I mentioned earlier and says, "Forget it—I'm not going along with this anymore."

Help for Pastoral Marriages

Because of all the pressures, then, we can find ourselves getting into one kind of rut or another. It can be a communication rut, an intimacy rut, or some other type of rut. And then our marriage isn't going anywhere, nor does it have any great benefit to either partner. Pastors and their spouses, though, are often the last ones to want to seek help. Let's face it: There's ego and loss of face involved. But then the choices are either business as usual—muddling through with a bad marriage— or divorce, with all its complications and problems.

How can we work instead to strengthen the relationship? Here are some proven ideas:

1. Model authenticity in following Christ, not image management

As I said, many marital problems in pastoral couples are the result of the pressure to have a perfect marriage. Since that's not possible, we put on a mask—we live a lie.

I call this "image management." There's a public self and a private self (which is normal, to a degree). The more our public self says one thing and our private self says something else, the more we have an image-management problem. And the more disparity there is between the two selves, the more internal tension we're going to feel.

When Cindy and I are strained out and I have to get up and give a message, I feel massive tension and internal stress. I'm thinking, *I'm being hypocritical.*

We need to admit we can't really model perfection. Only God is without sin. We can relate a lot to Peter, who wasn't perfect and who made mistakes. We should model authenticity as we're moving toward the goal of Christlikeness.

We need to be willing honestly to say, "I need to move forward in my relationship with my wife. Here are some of the things we've done as a couple to protect our relationship and move it forward." If we do that, people will cut us a lot of slack. They'll see that we're modeling authenticity for them—not just image management.

2. *Take charge of your schedule, and start scheduling for change*

If we don't set our schedule, somebody else will set it for us. That's especially true for the average pastor. There's always a group or a person within the church that wants to meet with him. There's always an outside group that has an idea for the church. That's one reason we get into ruts.

What's the solution? Recognize the important truth that more of the same will never bring change, and start taking charge of your own schedule (under God).

3. *Ask your wife how your marriage is doing*

I remember how I learned that my wife, Cindy, was frustrated with the state of our marriage at one point. I was an associate pastor at a large church, teaching couples about relationships. But then one day, we and two other couples were in a car together, and I said to Cindy (just trying to jump-start the conversation), "Cindy, tell me, how are we doing in our marriage on a scale of 1 to 10? In fact, let's all go around the car and rate our marriages. We'll start, okay, Cindy?"

She looked at me and kind of laughed.

I said, "No, come on, tell me."

"Do you really want to know?" she asked.

"Sure."

"Well, I think we're about a 4 right now."

Tension filled the car instantly. So I said, "Oh, lighten up. Come on, what is it really?"

Her silence communicated volumes. You can imagine what the atmosphere in the car was like by then!

As we dropped off the other two couples a while later, I was furious. "Oh, great!" I told her. "You just ruined all my credibility."

"John," she said, "if you don't want to know the answer to a question like that, don't ask me."

Talk about conviction! I was being an image-manager, not concerned about the truth of our situation. I asked her forgiveness and made a decision right then to move that 4 up to an 8—and I did!

We need to ask our wives how our marriages are doing.

4. Be a pioneer, not a settler

If your wife tells you your marriage is a 3 or a 4, or even a 5, on a 1 to 10 scale, take it as a warning flag. Don't say, "It'll go away. She'll work through it. It's just a stage."

It's not like teething! It really isn't "just a stage" in your marriage. When you begin to walk on thin ice, you've got a decision to make.

Let me draw a comparison from history. When our country was being settled, there were settlers and there were pioneers. The pioneers were the people who were always taking the arrows! They were forging ahead, doing new things. And the settlers were the people who were following after the pioneers, saying, "Is it safe out there?" If it was, the settlers would go out where the pioneers were, and the pioneers would move forward to new territory.

Well, guess who's being wiped out today in this changeable, high-stress time in our country? The pioneers (the people who are proactive, moving forward and saying, "Hey, let's take charge and forge ahead!") are no longer taking the arrows. It's the settlers who are getting wiped out in our economy and in relationships.

In other words, there's so much change, so much stress, that we can't just sit back anymore. We need to be pioneers and move forward toward God's best.

5. Set aside "recharging" time

Here's what I did with Cindy: I made a decision—quickly! I chose to be a pioneer. I said, "Cindy, let's be proactive." I called a friend to whom I had referred a hundred couples for counseling and asked, "Could we sit down with you for six weeks and just do an enrichment kind of thing? I don't know exactly what we'll talk about."

Cindy and I showed up at his office for the first session. It wasn't as if the wheels were coming off our marriage, but I wanted to do even better. So the counselor asked, "What are you here for?"

"Well, I don't know," I said. "Probably nothing. You'll probably refund our money after tonight! I doubt if we have anything to work on."

But my wife, of course, is very organized, and she had a whole checklist of things to discuss!

As it turned out, the experience was so good that every year now, in February, we go in for six sessions. We're committed to the truth found in Proverbs: "Only the wise seek counsel." I will die long before I run out of areas in which I can grow.

That's one way Cindy and I combat image management and focus on building a lasting love. For you it might be different. For example, our pastor carves out every Friday lunchtime in his busy schedule to take his wife to a quiet restaurant. They have a good time of communication there. He built the intimacy into his week. And they're doing great today because he has kept that Friday lunchtime inviolate for almost 20 years now.

All of us need to adopt an attitude that says, "Let's do something different! Let's change. Let's move forward in our relationship." Whether that means a regular time with a counselor, a weekly date, or some other option you think of, you've got to take time to be with your wife.

So often, we men speak a language of the head, while our wives speak a language of the heart. One person wants to talk feelings and emotions, and usually it's the wife, who's good at it. And then there's the other person who has a strong competitive streak (which drives us to success), and sometimes it's just hard for the wife to understand that drive in the male nature. These differences can create barriers to good communication.

When we get home from work, one or both of us is worn out. We come home to rest, not to relate. So we have to be intentional about developing a system for discussing things meaningfully. And that's where setting aside the time just for our wives comes in. That doesn't have to be a complex matter, either. Some couples can benefit greatly by going for a daily walk together; if you're out for a walk, the telephone isn't going to interrupt you.

For Cindy and me, besides our six counseling sessions in February, we also have a weekly date night. Every Tuesday night, for seven years without fail now, we overpay a college student to watch our kids while we concentrate on our relationship.

Whatever works best for you, make a commitment to spend regular, quality time with your wife. Listen to her; talk to her; really enter into some relational closeness.

6. *Remember that men and women are different: Put in discussion time*

Men and women are made differently. We think differently, we feel differently, and we're more sensitive in different areas. For example, it's easy to overlook the fact that women speak almost twice as many words in an average day as men do. The average man talks less, shares his feelings less, and is more competitive.

What does a pastor do during his average day? He solves problems, solves problems, and solves problems! When he hears an issue, he tends to go instantly to a solution. He pulls out a passage of Scripture, or he says, "Hey, let me pray for you." It's instantaneous.

But guess what? That average pastor could triple the impact of his marital communication by setting aside that tendency when it comes to his wife. When she brings up an issue, instead of going instantly to a solution, he should put in a time of discussion before offering suggestions. "Well, let's talk about that," he might say. "How does that make you feel? What do you mean by this?"

7. Make these new patterns habitual by becoming accountable for them

In the midst of the pastor's everyday stresses and strains, how can we keep all these things in mind? We have to make our new patterns of understanding and communication habitual. And to do that, it can help to have some cues to remind us.

Let me give you an example of what I mean. I used to point my finger at my kids when I was upset with them. (Of course, being in the ministry, I never got *angry* with my kids—I was just *emphatic.*) So, I'd be pointing at my kids and saying, "I can't believe you did that!"

Then, all of a sudden I realized, *This is terrible. It's ridiculous! I shouldn't be doing this*. So I spoke with my wife, and then I got both my kids together and said, "Okay, kids, I shouldn't be pointing my finger at you when I get upset. So from now on, any time I point my finger at you in anger, you instantly get a dollar."

Of course, you can imagine their little eyes! After that, they were deliberately provoking me to anger! And to my discredit, I lost about eight bucks the first week and a half. But I don't think I've lost two dollars in the year and a half since then. You know why? Because I made myself accountable for a change I wanted to see in my life.

The challenge for you, pastor—busy as you are—is to likewise make yourself accountable for how things are going in your life. A great way to do this is to get into a small group, where you and two or three other men will regularly ask one another the hard questions about the changes you want to make. For several years now, I've met with such a group every Tuesday morning.

Once again, you have to be the pioneer and not the settler. You have to ask yourself, *What can I do to interrupt some of the cycles in my life so that tomorrow isn't just more of the same? What can I do to bring about new things? What can I do that will really lead to positive change in my life?*

8. Take time to rest

Remember that the Lord Himself labored for six days and then rested on the seventh. One problem with us pastors is that we never take time to rest. We just lean forward the whole time, always keeping the bow bent, and that's a game plan for misery—certainly as far as a relationship with our wives goes!

At the end of the Song of Solomon, you see a wise woman saying to a busy king—her husband—"Let's go away, back to the vineyards and the fields where we fell in love at first."

That is so important. One reason we get into ruts is that we're doing so much for other people that we don't heed the words of Scripture to take a break, to rest, to recuperate. We never take a step back.

We need to be proactive about building into our schedules some time of refreshment with our wives.

9. Turn to Christ for help with your hurts

Many of us are in ministry today because we never got the Old Testament blessing from our fathers. I never did. There's an unbelievable hurt when you spend years repairing other people's relationships, and then your own dad cusses you out for doing what you do for a living (not to mention the pain of seeing him reject Christ at the end of his life).

Some of us, then, are looking to a congregation and/or our wives to fill that need for a blessing. Where we need to look is to the Lord Jesus Christ to deal with those hurts.

I'm sure all of us can relate in some way to having looked for our dad's approval or support and not finding it. And if we don't bring some resolution to the problems of the past that relate to our fathers, we're going to be hobbled in many ways as we try to live successfully in our homes.

A lot of you might be saying, "Oh, that doesn't affect me . . . affect me." Maybe you don't see the effect. But other people do. Maybe it slips out in that anger that comes only when you're in the car, driving by yourself.

Maybe it's that shortness with your family—you can treat everybody else nicer than you do the people in your own home. Why? Maybe (like me) you grew up with an angry father who never approved of you. And you've been out there, trying like crazy to please everybody else, not realizing what intimacy, love, and kindness at home are supposed to look like. It can be tough to duplicate what you've never seen.

So again it's time to say, "Lord, enough is enough. I want to be real and authentic. I don't want to be into image management; I don't want a public self and a private self that are different. I want to be wholly Your man, and that has to start at home. So may I be a man who really seeks to serve You and love You in every way. May I even face those difficult issues from the past. May I move forward in Christlikeness."

10. Come up with a tangible memorial marker

I would also encourage each pastor (and his wife) reading this chapter to come up with a tangible memorial marker of where you've been and where you want to go in life. What do I mean?

In the book of Joshua, after God led the people of Israel through the mighty river Jordan at flood stage, He said, "Go back and get some stones, and build a memorial to Me for what I have done." Now, the people had a lot of battles still ahead of them. They hadn't yet gone to Jericho. In fact, they had the whole conquest before them. Yet those rocks were a symbol to all of them—a memorial marker—of what God had done in their lives to that point and of where God could take them in the future.

Let me give you a quick example of a modern memorial marker. I worked with a pastoral couple not long ago whose major problem was image management. They looked great every Sunday, but they were "dukin' it out" Monday through Saturday. As they sat down and were honest enough to deal with some of the hurt, they came up with an interesting and appropriate memorial marker. They put a counterfeit dollar bill and a real dollar bill in a frame, and they hung that frame in their hallway, as well as another set in his office.

Nobody else who walks into their hallway may know exactly what those two dollar bills mean. But to that couple, it's a memorial marker that says, "We want to go forward with integrity. We want to be the real thing from here on out."

A memorial marker can be as simple as a rock. You could go into your backyard, get a rock, write the date on it, and put that rock on your desk. Nobody else needs to know what that date means except you and your wife. It could mean, "With God's help, we're going to move forward and have that date night!" or "With God's help, I'm going to move forward and begin not to have just an instantaneous reaction with my wife or my kids, but a discussion."

Moving Ahead

The ministry can become a demanding taskmaster that can take all your time away from your wife and your family. But I hope this discussion will convince you to be proactive about dealing with the problems and weak spots in your marriage.

As it says in Proverbs, "Without a plan, the people perish." It's time to realize you have to be a pioneer, to break new ground, to get a clear plan. For some of us, that might mean a date night. For others, it might mean sitting down with a counselor. And all of us would benefit from getting into a small group where we sit down together and say, "How are we doing?"

Just the process of saying, "I want my family to be a priority. Now, Honey, let's come up with a plan for how we're going to accomplish that this year" can be a great start. Do something tangible and bite-sized. That alone can bring an incredible amount of hope. Remember: More of the same will never bring change. Be a pioneer, not a settler!

Pastor *to* Pastor

Wow, what a chapter! As you can see, it's just loaded with practical, realistic ways for you to make your marriage better.

I want you to know that I continue to be concerned about pastors and their marriages. As I travel and meet with pastors, what I hear over and over is that you want help in keeping a good relationship with your wife and in being a good father. So, my friend, this chapter was for you! As is the next!

Why don't you take a minute, right now, and pray for God's guidance. Then do this: Go back to page 1 of this chapter so you can skim it and find least one area in which you can improve.

Then go to work on what God has shown you. Whether it's modeling authenticity rather than managing your image (John Trent's first suggested help) or coming up with a tangible memorial marker (his eleventh suggestion)—or one of the suggestions in between—take action! And may the Lord be your strength! God truly does want you to be a husband and a father after His own heart. No matter what your circumstances—no matter how hopeless things may look because of past conflicts with your spouse or mistakes in raising your kids—God wants you to keep going and to grow in your relationships with those very important people.

So, my friend, roll up your sleeves, say a prayer, and get to work! With the strength God provides, be the man God wants you to be. He will empower you!

H. B. L.

~ 5 ~

I want you to read a portion of a letter that made my heart sink when I received it. We had printed this correspondence before in the fifth issue of the "Pastor to Pastor" newsletter. It will point out to you once again some of the unique challenges we all face in ministry and how Satan will do all he can to divide us as clergy families.

> *After being a pastor's wife for 16 years, I thought I'd heard it all. But my husband came home the other evening from a pastor-parish meeting with a new one that smacked me between the eyes. Seems that this church we're serving is complaining now about our children. Our five-year-old son likes to stand with Daddy while Daddy shakes hands after church. People are complaining that a small boy has no place standing there when people want to talk with the pastor. My husband was told, "You can be a father on your own time. When you're here at church, you're here to serve us!" One man even said, "I wouldn't even think of taking my child to work with me."*
>
> *My husband and I decided that maybe it would just be best for a while if the children and I left immediately after the conclusion of the service, so no children would offend the parishioners. Now I'm being criticized for not being friendly and for "running out the door" as if I don't care for anyone.*

Another pastor's wife of 36 years wrote me: "The 'Pastor to Pastor' series has been of great encouragement in this stage of my life. My husband is a very caring, people-centered person, and is 'on-call' both at church and at home. I find I must have 'time out' for a segment of time during the week. . . . I am frustrated if my husband does not take time away from the church for us to focus on our lives and home."

Attention! Attention! Attention! We all need to feel as though we matter to one another, especially in the minister's home. Dennis Rainey does a wonderful job of making that point and then leading us toward a positive solution.

I've had the privilege of being a guest on Dennis's radio program, "Family Life Today." He's a gentle, genial host with so much love to offer those he meets along the way. The thing that most impressed me as I talked with Dennis was how he valued and honored his wife and children. See if you don't feel the same way as you follow his guidance in this insightful chapter.

H. B. London Jr.

Growing Together as Husband and Wife

by Dennis Rainey

The other day, I went home to work because I couldn't get any work done at the office. When I walked into the house, my wife, Barbara, said, "I want you to look at the playroom and see how I've scrubbed the carpet." She added, "I worked on my hands and knees for 90 minutes."

Standing in the playroom with my wife, I looked at the floor and made a typical, true-male reply: "I *knew* we chose the wrong color of carpet for this room when we picked it out."

"That's not what I wanted to hear," she said. "I wanted to hear that you appreciated my working so hard to keep our house presentable."

Oh, how easily problems in marriage can arise!

What had I done? I had gone straight to the bottom line. I had reviewed our choice of carpet (in which I had played a part, by the way) and "thrown a verbal stone" at her. And my not thinking cost me! My wife's jaw got a little tight, and so did mine.

How about you? How's your marriage going?

Frequently, pastors' marriages are the ones most in need of counseling. They need to talk to somebody who can open a few doors and turn on some lights for them. A 1992 article in *Leadership* journal pointed out that 81 percent of the pastoral couples responding to a survey felt they have insufficient time together. In fact, they looked at this as their number-one problem—ahead of the use of money, income level, communication difficulties, differences over the use of time off, difficulties in rearing children, sexual problems, and anger.

Forty-nine percent of the pastors in the survey (virtually one out of two) indicated they and their spouse desire more frequent sexual intimacy; only 10 percent felt very satisfied with the current level. They talked a lot about time problems, night meetings, and pressures in the church.

How can pastors feel good about tutoring others when they themselves aren't doing well in Marriage 101?

Communication

The Problem

In my opening illustration, a key problem for Barbara and me was in our communication. Why is good communication often so difficult—even among those of us who instruct other people in how to talk with their mates?

First, think of the context in which we are professional communicators. We deliver monologues from a pulpit! And we listen to people all the time, but we listen to them after we preach or in a counseling session where it's very intense. We're communicators, all right, but we're trained to exposit the Bible and illustrate a sermon. We're not trained to listen to, understand, and communicate with the opposite sex.

When I went to seminary, I took a class in interpersonal communication. It was interesting, but it was almost all theory and no lab. There were no assignments for us to apply what we were learning by relating with another person.

Second, pastors can be (and often are) exhausted from ministry by the time they get home at night. When it comes to be bedtime, after ministering hard all day, they are simply exhausted. Haven't we all been too tired to work things out with our wives? So we say, "Forget it; I'm just going to go to sleep." But if we do that enough nights in a row, we're going to be emotionally divorced from our wives, emotionally isolated from each other.

Third, most of us aren't skilled in resolving conflicts in our own marriages. We may know how to resolve them between two parties who sit in our office. But often we don't know how to sit down with our spouse and say, "I'm sorry." Nor do we know how to listen to her and say, "You're right; I haven't been making you a priority. I haven't made you my disciple. I'm not praying with you."

We can be guilty of ignoring the obvious: A pastor's number-one disciple, friend, ally, and partner in life is his wife. But unless he comes alongside her and treats her accordingly, their relationship is not going to blossom. Instead, there's going to be the feeling that you're missing each other, that you just don't seem able to connect.

The Solution

When you add together those three elements that hinder our communication, all of a sudden you have a combustible mixture that can lead to a marital meltdown. What's the solution?

First, you need to make a commitment to communicate with your wife. Put her on your prayer list. Pray for her every morning in your devotions. Ask the Lord to help you bring about better communication between you and your wife.

Second, admit you're human and that you and your wife are going to "miss" each other from time to time. Confess the obvious. If you're one of those men who has almost never said to his wife, "I'm sorry," the

Anonymous

Dear Focus on the Family,

Last Sunday, I was reminded that my feet are still clay. Usually, I find the flirtation of women other than my wife to be offensive. The last 4 weeks have been most demanding. I put in 76, 64, 59, and 49 hours, respectively. Needless to say, I have neglected and been neglected at home. The positive feedback from my wife was low. No hostility, no arguments, no fights—just simply autopilot.

Sunday, an attractive young lady asked to head up a major project in the church. She also commented on what a wonderful pastor I was. She flirts with everyone in sight, and usually I find it kind of repulsive. But this Sunday, I found it somewhat exciting. Even more than that, I found that she kept coming to mind, and that bothered me very much.

I took the time on Tuesday to make myself accountable to three people—including another pastor I deeply respect. I confessed openly and asked them to hold me accountable. They will call me at unexpected times

simple fact is that you need to add those words to your vocabulary.

Third, when you have a conflict with your wife, you must not settle for isolation but find a way to work it out.

Barbara and I have learned to do something that helps our communication more than anything else: We end every day by praying together right before we go to sleep. It's not a long prayer—sometimes it's just an acknowledgment of the lordship of Jesus Christ and a thank you for the day. We might pray for the challenges of the day, for an urgent need, or for the needs of our kids. In nearly 25 years of marriage, we've failed to pray together less than a dozen times.

No discipline or ritual has enhanced our relationship more than this simple pattern of praying together before bed. Why? You can't pray with somebody you're angry with. This spiritual discipline can force you to communicate! You have to work it through and not stay mad at the other person.

Fourth—and this is going to be difficult for many of us men—if you can't find a way to work out a particular problem with your wife, you need to get a third party (perhaps another pastor or a counselor) to coach you in working it out together.

Fifth, you need to fear God. Let me explain.

In 1 Corinthians 9:27, Paul gave us a warning: "Lest possibly I, after having preached the gospel to others, might be disqualified." We know that passage isn't talking about not making it to heaven; it *is* talking about being disqualified and called unworthy of ministry. And this is a big motivation to me: to think about the possibility that *Yes, I could be disqualified.*

I've seen it happen. I've stopped counting after 45 names on a list I kept for a number of years—a list of men whose ministries are finished for all practical purposes because they didn't maintain the spiritual thread of commitment to Jesus Christ and their wives. *They didn't keep their marriage vows. They didn't fear God.*

So we need to say, "Lord, I'm going to fear You. I'm going to fulfill my ordination vows, and I'm going to fulfill my marriage vows, even though sometimes I don't feel like it. Even when the easiest thing for me to do would be to escape and hide, I'm going to fulfill my covenants. Even when the easiest thing would be to hook up with somebody who 'better understands me,' I'm going to be faithful to my promises."

One of the real dangers of the ministry is that we're exposed to many women we can hook up with emotionally. But if we give in to the temptation, we fall into "emotional adultery." It can happen in a prayer meeting or a counseling session. Before we know it, we're snared, trapped. I believe those of us in ministry today need to make a fresh commitment to learn to fear God (see Prov. 2).

every week and ask me hard questions. Second, I took my wife to lunch, and we talked. She had experienced similar things, and we decided on the following: one, never work more than 55 hours a week; two, a date each week, no matter what; three, open conversation about attractions; four, our new, young church worker is placed under the leadership of an older elder.

It's not over and done, but your broadcast was a big help. I ask you to pray for us. And I say, "Thank you."

The Special Vulnerability of Pastoral Life

The need for fearing God and for fulfilling our covenant with our wives leads me to think about the special vulnerability to infidelity that pastors face because of their ministerial duties.

The Problem

Ministry addiction. For one thing, the pastorate can become an addiction. I call it the ministry addiction. It feeds a man's need for significance.

I don't really understand all I know about this, but I've seen a lot of pastors who never comprehend the cycle of their year. They don't realize when their down points are or when they're going to be exhausted. So they go through a near burnout over and over, until many of them get caught emotionally and slip off into some secret sin because they are weakened.

When such a pastor is finally found out, some might say, "Well, he's not a man of conviction. He doesn't have character." But I think there's a deficiency in his personality so that he tries to find satisfaction and significance in the wrong place.

Isolation and friendlessness. The pastorate also tends to isolate. It keeps a pastor and his wife from developing normal, everyday, run-of-the-mill relationships. A pastor can find it difficult to establish and maintain meaningful friendships. And isolation can lead to additional problems.

Emotional vulnerability. When you minister to a member of the opposite sex *spiritually*, you are touching her soul, her *emotions*. And at the same time, *your* emotions can get involved. That's why we see pastors falling into adultery: Most physically adulterous relationships begin as emotional adultery. It starts in the area of spiritual ministry—which touches on this core issue of who we are and on our pastoral duty to minister to our flock.

I believe many pastors who fall morally are trying to find the fulfillment of a need that just isn't being filled in their marital lives. It begins in seminary, with its great pressures and costs. The demand is on the husband to get trained theologically for the pastorate. This produces a man who develops spiritually while he leaves his wife in the dust, so to speak.

When this man then turns around to grab his wife's hand after graduation, he finds he's married to a virtual stranger, spiritually speaking. So when he marches off to the church and the spiritual battle, he is vulnerable to downfall if he tries to meet his own emotional needs by reaching out to women he counsels.

The Solution

How do we deal with this problem? First, you need to understand that you are vulnerable because of your spiritual role in other women's lives—and pray accordingly.

Second, at whatever point you are in your marriage, you need to start discipling your wife so that both she and you can have your spiritual *and* emotional needs met through each other.

Third, you should develop healthy friendships with other couples. However tight your schedule is, you absolutely need time for these friendships: first with your wife, then with other couples. These friendships are not an option.

Pastors need to be real, authentic—to drop their guard with their friends. A lot of pastors are scared to be truly honest. They think the laity will lose respect for them if they're human.

Personally, I've found that such open relationships are not easy to come by. The devil seems to throw everything in the book at us to keep us from getting that time with a person of kindred spirit—someone who's on our side and who's not picking on us but encouraging us. I've had several disappointments in this area over my years in the ministry. At points I've wondered if it's worth it to pursue those relationships, because they really don't come without a great cost. But they are crucial if you and I are to run the race that is set before us.

For us as pastors, though, our friendships are essential not just for the survival of our marriages, but also so that our marriages will stay on the cutting edge and flourish through many fruitful years of ministry.

Sex

As I mentioned earlier, according to a survey done by *Leadership*, 49 percent of the pastors indicated that they and their wives desire more frequent sexual intimacy. They use a lot of excuses for why it isn't better. But the end result is that they've reached a point in their marriages where they just don't have the time or energy for sex, and so they struggle with a great deal of dissatisfaction.

It begins when we lose touch emotionally with each other. Even though we're surrounded by spiritual teachings, *we don't grow together spiritually*. Next, because we're not developing intimacy in those areas, we begin to "disconnect" with each other. A relationship that isn't growing will stagnate and slowly die.

The solution to this problem begins with you taking responsibility to meet your wife's needs. And what are those needs? She wants tenderness, affection, and conversation. She wants a relationship. She wants to feel like a partner.

If her husband is being pulled to a meeting on this night, another meeting the next night, a third meeting the third night (so that he always gets home late and exhausted), he doesn't have anything left to share with her when he gets home.

So we end up (if we're not careful) not being *partners* in life. But as 1 Peter 3:7 tells husbands, "Grant her honor as a fellow heir"—as a partner, as the woman who shares life with us.

Early in our marriage, some of Barbara's weaknesses began to irritate me. I'm not proud to admit this, but I felt she was starting to be a limitation to me, a hindrance to my ability to accomplish (of all things!) God's work. I had to pull back, look at my wife with fresh eyes, and ask, "Am I going to view my wife as an obstruction in her weaknesses, or am I going to believe the truth: that God knew what He was doing when He gave me my wife—that Barbara, in her weaknesses and in her strengths, is God's personal selection for me?"

When I decided I was not going to resent Barbara for her weaknesses but instead embrace her in the totality of who she was and adjust my schedule to her need for me to be at home, that became the fork in the road that made it possible for us to have a true partnership now some 25 years later.

We also need to talk about a man's needs. I don't agree with everything in Dr. Willard Harley's book *His Needs, Her Needs*, but I was interested in a survey he took of some 2,200 clients. It revealed that a man's number-one need is sexual fulfillment. It's the wise pastor's wife who knows how to meet her husband's need in this area.

First Corinthians 7 says there's only one reason for married people to abstain temporarily from sexual intercourse: higher, spiritual intercourse (communion) with God. The regular coming together of the pastor and his wife in a spirit of contagious romance is a must.

To accomplish this, a pastor and his wife need to rethink their priorities, take time to cultivate their relationship, and find ways to reignite romance. Dealing with sex may mean seeking out and getting some advice. Maybe it means telling a close friend that you're struggling in this area and you would like him to pray for you.

But—so that I'm not misunderstood—for a man, that close friend must always be another man. Never, *never* admit to anyone of the opposite sex that you have a sexual struggle—not even to someone you work with in your ministry or on your staff, someone you're counseling, or anyone in your church. To do so guarantees sexual chemistry.

We men are bottom-line oriented. We want to go for the objective. We know what we want. But that's not how our wives are wired. So we men have to pull back from the urgency of what we're feeling.

And right here is where the words of Christ come in. He calls us to servant leadership (see Mark 10:35-45). He calls us to die to self.

Now, I have to admit that I've been out jogging at times, saying to the Lord, "Lord, I don't like this death-to-self stuff. I'd much rather she die to herself and meet my needs." But the Scripture begins with the man: He's the head of his wife as Christ is the head of the church (see Eph. 5).

Thus, we men need to start with ourselves and not with our wives. We've got to get our feet off our wife's neck and stop preaching to her, and instead we have to decide what our responsibility is.

The Need for Romance

Oswald Chambers once said, "Human nature, if it is healthy, demands excitement. And if it does not obtain its thrilling excitement in the right way, it will seek it in the wrong. God never made bloodless stoics; He makes passionate saints."

I love that quotation! I'm passionate about Jesus' kingdom, and I'm passionate about my wife. I love her. I want a relationship with her that will handle the challenges of her health issues. (She's had heart surgery and has nearly died on four different occasions.) I want to share life with her as we raise our kids and build the ministry God has chosen for us.

But do you know what else I want? I want some romance with her.

We've found that there are two enemies of romance. One is *boredom and predictability*. To battle this, we kicked our romance into a new gear several years ago. We got away together for three nights to unplug from the ministry and the family, to refresh and renew our relationship, and to enjoy some sexual pleasure.

I don't believe God frowns on that. Instead, what we did enables us to handle the second enemy of romance—*pressure and fatigue*.

We found that two nights was not enough; we needed three. That way, we could fall into bed exhausted the first night and still have a couple of days left to share and talk.

Another thing I encourage couples to do is to think back to those things that originally brought sparks to your relationship. What did you do to court each other? What have been the three most romantic times in all your marriage? Barbara and I revisit those, because in those memories are some secrets to maintaining romance today.

Courtship demands time, focus, and a relationship that's being refreshed and renewed. And it takes getting away for a long weekend to do that! We try to get away three times a year for a minimum of three nights each time. I encourage pastors—especially those with young children—to get away four times a year. It's absolutely essential.

Developing Respect

In successful marriages, the partners have *mutual respect*, which is the basis of all good relationships. If you think about it, that's how God asked us to start out with Him in the Old Testament: He commanded us to respect, fear, and reverence Him, to set Him apart. And that's how we have to operate in our human relationships.

It's so easy for a husband and wife to take each other for granted. So many marriages—especially in the ministry—come to a place not of divorce, but of having no emotional connection anymore. The pastor and his wife are like ships passing in the night.

How can we cultivate mutual respect for one another?

Begin with making a spiritual commitment. The most precious possession Barbara and I own is a document we wrote in our first year of marriage. Together, we signed over the title deed of our lives to God. We made a spiritual commitment to each other then, which has been helpful to review. Those ragged pages we signed so long ago remind us of who really holds the title to our lives.

Communication may be down in a marriage for a time. One spouse may be upset with the other. But we've always got our marriage vows and our covenant—our commitment to Christ and to each other that we will keep our relationship intact regardless of whatever else happens.

Be teachable. Commit to learning from God and each other. This includes admitting faults, asking forgiveness, learning lessons, seeking advice, giving each other access into one another's life, and being accountable to each other.

Make your marriage a priority. Meet each other's needs. Don't give just lip service to this thing called Christian marriage, but instead let others see you setting your marriage apart in specific ways.

Barbara and I always have a weekly date night. We go to a certain family restaurant that's noisy, and we pull out a notepad, our calendars, and our priority lists. Then we talk to each other about issues.

The other day, a waiter and waitress came to our table and said, "Where have you guys been?" (We'd been traveling and hadn't been to the restaurant for two or three weeks.) They added, "We're concerned about you. Are you guys okay?"

We laughed and answered, "Yeah, we're okay. Why?"

"Well, you are kind of our model."

It's flattering to have somebody call you a model. I don't ever think of myself in those terms.

You see, Barbara and I are just hammering out life and trying to follow Jesus as best we know how. Little did we know that a waiter and waitress were watching carefully what we were doing.

One of the best ways we can have family-centered churches is for pastors, in their heart of hearts, to be marriage- and family-centered in their own schedules and their own calendars week in and week out.

Now is the time in our private lives to be making the priorities of marriage and family truly work.

Pastor *to* Pastor

To all you pastors and pastors' wives who have just finished this chapter by Dennis Rainey, I want to say that if it troubles you, then get away from the hubbub, all the noise of the family and the kids, the television set, and any other distractions, and go walking somewhere together. Allow your minds to race back to the beginning days of your marriage and all the dreams and aspirations you had for your ministry. Recount some of them to each other. Relive some past moments, and take a minute to say, "I really love you. I thank you for standing by me through all this. We're in this thing together. My ministry would not have been nearly as successful had it not been for your encouragement, your prayers, your love—and for your just being you! I want to thank you for being my partner in this. We have been a blessing to others because in so many ways, we've blessed each other."

Do it, my friend. Do it! Ministry responsibilities will wait another few hours. We can so glibly state that our priorities are God, then wife and family, and finally church. Now's the time to put those priorities into action, pastor! Take your wife by the hand, and go for that walk. Just be together for a while.

I wish I had done it more often.

H. B. L.

∽ 6 ∾

A few months ago, while in Israel, Beverley and I were invited to spend the Sabbath with a Jewish family. They weren't Christians, I might add, and were very committed to the Jewish lifestyle. The experience for both of us was one we shall not soon forget.

On Friday afternoon, life in Israel comes to a calculated slowdown for many. Families leave work early, make their way to their homes, park their cars, and for nearly 24 hours commit themselves to one another and to rest. They usually begin the period with a big meal—attended by extended family members—and then they fellowship and relax. Only on a rare occasion will anything work-related disturb the tranquillity of their rest. Beverley and I marveled at this wonderful custom, especially in light of the fact that for three decades, we allowed so many outside influences to disrupt "our time alone"—"our day off."

The following chapter entitled "The Pastor's Sabbath" was not a part of "Pastor to Pastor." Rather, it's a reprint of an article by Eugene Peterson that appeared in Christianity Today. *Perhaps you've read it before. Even if you have, however, I submit that it's well worth your reading again.*

What Eugene has to say to us may seem extreme at first—especially in light of the massive expectations upon you and your family—but what if you could take just a suggestion or two from him and apply it to your home and family? What if you would gradually give yourself the permission to live out the real meaning of Sabbath? Please give it a try!

H. B. London Jr.

The Pastor's Sabbath

by Eugene H. Peterson

Many people simply cannot believe there can be a large, leisurely center to life where God can be pondered. They doubt they can enter realms of spirit where wonder and adoration have a place to develop, and where play and delight have time to flourish. Is all this possible in our fast-paced lives?

I began asking this question out of my own life as a pastor. But I was soon asking the question out of the circumstances of my friends and parishioners, putting myself in their shoes, their ways of life, their vocations.

I decided that it is possible. It's possible because there is a biblical provision for it. The name for it is Sabbath.

An accurate understanding of Sabbath is prerequisite to its practice: It must be understood biblically, not culturally. A widespread misunderstanding of Sabbath trivializes it by designating it "a day off." "A day off" is a bastard Sabbath. Days off are not without benefits, to be sure, but Sabbaths they are not. However beneficial, they're not a true, but a secularized, Sabbath. The motivation is utilitarian: It makes us feel better. Relationships improve. We may even get more done on the six working days. The purpose is to restore strength, increase motivation, and keep performance incentives high.

Sabbath means quit. Stop. Take a break. Cool it. The word itself has nothing devout or holy in it. It's a word about time, denoting our nonuse of it—what we usually call wasting time.

The biblical context for understanding Sabbath is the Genesis week. Sabbath is the seventh and final day in which God "rested [sabbath] from all the work of creating that he had done" (Gen. 2:3). We can learn from that sequence of days in which God spoke energy and matter into existence. We can also learn from the repeated refrain, "And there was evening and there was morning, one day . . . and there was evening and there was morning"—on and on, six times.

This is the Hebrew way of understanding day; it is not ours. American days—most of them, anyway—begin with an alarm clock ripping the predawn darkness. They close, not with evening, but several hours past that when we turn off the electric light. In conventional references to day, we do not include the night hours except for the two or three we steal from either end to give us more time to work. Because our definition of day is so different, we have to make an imaginative effort to understand the Hebrew phrase "evening and morning, one day."

Beginning with Quitting

More than idiomatic speech is involved here; there is a sense of rhythm. Day is the basic unit of God's creative work; evening is the beginning of that day. It's the onset of God speaking light, stars, earth, vegetation, animals, man, and woman into being. But it's also the time when we quit our activity and go to sleep. When it is evening, "I lay me down to sleep and pray the Lord my soul to keep" and drift off into unconsciousness for the next 6 or 8 or 10 hours, a state in which I am absolutely nonproductive.

Then I wake up, rested, jump out of bed full of energy, grab a cup of coffee, and rush out the door to get things started. The first thing I discover (a great blow to the ego) is that everything was started hours—centuries—ago! While I was fast asleep—before I was even born—all the important things were set in motion. When I dash into the workday, I walk into a world in which God has been at work, an operation that is half over already. I enter into work in which the basic plan is already established, the assignments given, the operations underway.

The Hebrew evening/morning sequence conditions us to the rhythms of grace. We go to sleep, and God begins His work. As we sleep, He develops His covenant. We wake and are called out to participate in God's creative action. We respond in faith, in work. But always grace is previous. Grace is primary. We wake into a world we did not make, into a salvation we did not earn. Evening: God begins, without our help, His creative day. Morning: God calls us to enjoy and share and develop the work He initiated. Creation and covenant are sheer grace and there to greet us every morning. George MacDonald once wrote that sleep is God's contrivance for giving us the help He cannot get into us when we're awake.

I read and reread these opening pages of Genesis, along with certain sequences of Psalms, and recover these deep, elemental rhythms, internalizing the reality in which the strong, initial pulse is God's creating/saving word, God's providential/sustaining presence, God's grace.

As this biblical Genesis rhythm works in me, I also discover something else: When I quit my day's work, nothing essential stops. I prepare for sleep not with a feeling of exhausted frustration because there is so much yet undone and unfinished, but with expectancy. The day is about to begin! God's genesis words are about to be spoken again. During the hours of my sleep, how will He prepare to use my obedience, service, and speech when morning breaks? I go to sleep to get out of the way for a while. I get into the rhythm of salvation. While we sleep, great and marvelous things, far beyond our capacities to invent or engineer, are in process—the moon marking the seasons, the lion roaring before its prey, the earthworms aerating the earth, the proteins repairing our muscles, our dreaming brains restoring a deeper sanity beneath the gossip and scheming of our waking hours. Our work settles into the context of God's work. Human effort is honored and respected not as a thing in itself, but by its integration into the rhythms of grace and blessing.

Sabbath extrapolates this basic, daily rhythm into the larger context of the month. The turning of the earth on its axis gives us the basic two-beat rhythm, evening/morning. The moon in its orbit introduces another rhythm, the 28-day month, marked by 4 phases of 7 days each. It is this larger rhythm, the rhythm of the seventh day, that we are commanded to observe. Sabbath-keeping presumes the daily rhythm, evening/morning.

We can hardly avoid stopping our work each night as fatigue and sleep overtake us. But we can avoid stopping work on the seventh day, especially if things are gaining momentum. Keeping the weekly rhythm requires deliberate action. Sabbath-keeping often feels like an interruption, an interference with our routines. It challenges assumptions we gradually build up that our daily work is indispensable in making the world go. And then we find it's not an interruption but a more spacious rhythmic measure that confirms and extends the basic beat. Every seventh day, a deeper note is struck—an enormous gong whose deep sounds reverberate under and over and around the daily timpani percussions of evening/morning, evening/morning: creation honored and contemplated, redemption remembered and shared.

Pray and Play

In the two biblical versions of the Sabbath commandment, the commands are identical but the supporting reasons differ. The Exodus reason is that we are to keep the Sabbath because God kept it (see Exod. 20:8-11). God did His work in six days and then rested. If God sets apart one day to rest, we can, too. The work/rest rhythm is built into the very structure of God's interpenetration of reality. The precedent to quit doing and simply be is divine.

The Deuteronomy reason for Sabbath-keeping is that our ancestors in Egypt went 400 years without a vacation (see Deut. 5:15)—never a day off. The consequence: They were no longer considered persons but slaves, hands, work units—not persons created in the image of God but equipment for making bricks and building pyramids. Humanity was defaced.

Lest any of us do that to our neighbor, husband, wife, child, or employee, we are commanded to keep a Sabbath. The moment we begin to see others in terms of what they can do rather than who they are, we mutilate humanity and violate community. It's no use claiming, "I don't need to rest this week and therefore will not keep a Sabbath"; our lives are so interconnected that we inevitably involve others in our work whether we intend it or not. Sabbath-keeping is elemental kindness. Sabbath-keeping is commanded to preserve the image of God in our neighbors so that we see them as they are, not as we need them or want them.

The two biblical reasons for Sabbath-keeping develop into parallel Sabbath activities of praying and playing. The Exodus reason directs us to the contemplation of God, which becomes prayer and worship. The Deuteronomy reason directs us to social leisure, which becomes play. Praying and playing are deeply congruent with each other and have extensive inner connection.

Being Full by Being Spare

For 18 years, Monday was my Sabbath. Nothing was scheduled for Mondays. If emergencies arose, I responded, but there were surprisingly few. My wife joined me in observing the day. We made a lunch, put it in a day pack, took our binoculars, and drove anywhere from 15 minutes to an hour away to a trailhead along a river or into the mountains. Before we began our hike, my wife read a psalm and prayed. After that prayer, we did no more talking—we entered into a silence that continued for the next two or three hours, until we stopped for lunch.

We walked leisurely, emptying ourselves, opening ourselves to what was there: fern shapes, flower fragrance, bird song, granite outcropping, oaks and sycamores, rain, snow, sleet, wind. We had clothes for all kinds of weather and so never canceled our Sabbath-keeping because of weather any more than our Sunday churchgoing—and for the same reason: We needed our Sabbath just as much as our parishioners needed theirs. When the sun or our stomachs told us it was lunchtime, we broke the silence with a prayer of blessing for the sandwiches and fruit, the river and the forest. We were free to talk then, sharing bird sightings, thoughts, observations, ideas—however much or little we were inclined.

We returned home in the middle or late afternoon, puttered, did odd jobs, read. After supper, I usually wrote family letters. That was it: no Sinai thunder, no Damascus Road illuminations, no Patmos visions. It was a day set apart for solitude and silence, for "not doing," for being there. It was the sanctification of time.

We didn't have any rules for preserving the sanctity of the day, only the commitment that it be set apart for being, not using.

My wife kept, off and on, a Sabbath journal for the 18 years we did this. You would not be greatly impressed, I think, if you read the sporadic entries: bird lists, wildflowers in bloom, snatches of conversation, brief notes on the weather. But the spareness records a fullness, a presence. For Sabbath-keeping is not primarily something we do, but what we don't do.

Recently, my work changed from pastor to professor. We moved across the continent from Maryland to British Columbia. With that change, it became possible to keep a more conventional Sabbath. When I enter the church now, I no longer head for the pulpit; rather, my wife and I take our places in a pew on Sunday mornings and worship with a congregation of Christians.

Outwardly, it's a radical change. Instead of carrying binoculars, we hold a hymnbook in our hands; instead of listening to warblers, we listen to the choir; instead of lunching on tuna sandwiches, we feast on the sacrament. But our Sabbath in the sanctuary is in some ways not much different from what it was in the woods. We enter a world of prayer, we loosen our grip, we don't say much; we mostly listen and receive; we set the world and ourselves aside and cultivate attentive leisure before God.

But there's one striking difference—community. We are now in the Sabbath company of children and men and women, greeting and being greeted by Africans and Canadians and Japanese. There's an element of festivity here that we never had walking alone on the forest trails.

This celebrative element has been accentuated for us in an unexpected way. After the benediction in worship, we often go home, get some bread and fruit, and walk a couple of miles to Vancouver's celebrated beaches and sea wall to eat our lunch. The place is alive with walkers and bicyclists, kite flyers and beachcombers, grandparents and children and parents, kayaks and sailboats, laughter and games and picnicking. The outdoor playfulness always strikes a chord of harmonious response in our hearts that have been so recently tuned to prayerfulness in the sanctuary.

Vancouver is notorious for its non-churchgoing, but at least these people seem to know half of what Sunday means: "Quit your ordinary work; celebrate the creation; enjoy your family and friends!" North Americans are more used to observing obsessive Sunday shopping or addictive Sunday working among those who don't go to church (also among some who do). We have never before been among so many people who treat Sunday with such exuberant delight. This city plays on Sunday.

But I'm glad we don't have to settle for only half.

Pastor *to* Pastor

Two ideas seem to come out time after time in the chapters of this book. The first is your need as a pastor to have a friend, a mentor, an accountability person or group, a peer group. Call it what you will, but whatever variation it takes, you—we—need it!

And the second is the concept of balance between your work and your time "off." This is the need Eugene Peterson addresses so wonderfully in the chapter you've just read. You need time to pray and to play.

God did not design you to work seven days a week, week after week. If you are, you need to talk to your board—your elders, deacons, or vestry—and have them help you get the "fiscal Lord's day" that you need.

I recall one frustrated pastor writing to me, "The issue I believe that church people—pastors and laymen—need to hear from you is boundaries. The pastor and the people need to realize that the pastor does not solve their problems. We are not God, and we are not omnipotent."

A pastor's wife, when asked what topic she would choose for a seminary course for future clergy wives, responded with one word, "boundaries." When asked what the title of that course would be, she said, "Build Your Fence Where You Want It." She's right on target, isn't she?

In your life, pastor, there will always be another phone call to make, another parishioner to visit, a sermon to prepare, a talk to give, a funeral to conduct, a wedding to perform—not to mention a family to manage—the list is endless.

You need time away with your family, as well as time alone with God. One popular minister in the United States compares many pastors to "wagons with their wheels coming off, heading for the ditch."

My friend, take Eugene Peterson's advice. Take that day off as a Sabbath in order to pray and play. You need that day of rest. Please set it and keep it!

H. B. L.

7

As I think back over the nearly four years of producing "Pastor to Pastor" at the time of this writing, one of the most successful and referenced editions is the one we did on "Learning to Lead," and especially the segment featuring the wisdom of author and consultant Bobb Biehl. It was one of our earliest attempts to come alongside pastors and their families. And what made the edition so meaningful was the 10 questions he raised. Those questions form the foundation of the next chapter.

I will almost guarantee you that when you can give an answer to many or all of those questions, you can change the way you do ministry if you care to.

I remember one pastor writing us after hearing the "Pastor to Pastor" edition with Bobb. He said, "Today I finished listening and listened again to your interview with Bobb Biehl, this time with pen and paper to respond to the 10 questions he suggested." I hope that before too many days pass, you will do the same and put your own personal spin on what you read and glean in the next few pages.

Bobb Biehl is a member of the board of directors at Focus on the Family. He has been a valued resource for all of us in the ministry for many years. His latest book, Mentoring, *is a must read for all of you.*

H. B. London Jr.

Ten Questions to Focus Your Time for the Rest of Your Life

by Bobb Biehl

Consider the following letter:

My number-one challenge is filling the various hats I have to wear. In a given seven-day period, I meet preschoolers, elementary-age [children], junior- and senior-high [students]; counsel messed-up teens; joke together with teens; guide young singles; provide premarital counsel; do weddings and funerals; visit people in prison or the hospital or a nursing home; keep in touch with the day-to-day needs of people in our church; handle church administration and finance; create a meaningful, relevant, biblical sermon that fits in the right time of the year and will speak to people who attend our service ranging in age from 1 to 91 years of age; coordinate the worship service; provide commu-

> nity functions; remain current in social issues and help guide our church to be involved in a certain issue; [and] spend time rescuing people from their sins, sexual problems of all kinds, rape, child abuse, surrogate parenting, dysfunction in marriage, homosexuality, sex education. Additions to this would include dealing with those who are addicted to drugs and alcohol, addictions to laziness (and to work), anorexia, anger and rage, stunted personality development, low self-esteem, and hopelessness. It is impossible to be competent in all these areas, and yet that's the reality of my job. And those tasks don't even include my family responsibilities and my personal and spiritual needs.

Could you have written that letter? The writer might have exaggerated his week's activities, but he certainly didn't overstate his emotions. That pastor feels the way many pastors do: as if he's drowning in responsibilities. And then some of us are perfectionistic, so we feel we have to do all those things perfectly—in addition to the standard feeling that we have to do all those things all the time!

Each person mentioned above—as well as the pastor himself—wants him to have all the answers. But a pastor has to retreat at certain points to "I don't know." You can't be the Answer Man to every person at all levels at all times. You have to be able to say in some cases, "I don't know, but I love you, and I'll pray for you. Right now, though, I just don't have the answer."

As a consultant, I run into the same thing. People pay me well to be the Answer Man. Occasionally, though, I have to look at a person and say, "My heart hurts with you, and I wish I could give you a simple answer. But I just don't know. There isn't an answer to your situation that's obvious to me at the moment." There's a sense in which you, like me, have to have a lot more love than you have answers.

Asking Questions

I concluded early in life that no problem has ever been solved without asking questions. So I decided about 20 years ago that the better you get at asking the right questions, the better your chances are of solving the problem you're facing. That's why, when I consult with a pastor, whether he has a large paid staff or a volunteer team, I ask a lot of questions. In this chapter, I'm going to address the 10 most important ones.

Since so many of you have the problem of feeling overwhelmed by your schedule, the congregation's expectations and responsibilities, and your own perfectionistic tendencies, the key to the solution is to ask yourself questions that can clear your head about what the next steps might be. That's what these 10 questions can do for you.

Getting Away to Think

A lot of people don't have a system to help them refocus their life and energies. They have some time when they get away, but they don't know what questions to ask themselves when they take that retreat.

The following 10 questions will help you get that focus no matter what point in life you're at. And they'll still be useful 10, 20, and 30 years from now. So take the questions and get a day away, as Jesus did often to refocus His thoughts when He was under all the pressure. He went into the mountains and into the desert.

These questions will help you get the big picture of what you're about as a pastor and where you go from here.

How to Begin Your Retreat

A lot of us have good intentions about taking a retreat. But when we do it, we're like the little bird that just sits and stares. We don't think, and we don't come back refocused. We just keep going on the same old treadmill, getting more and more frustrated.

The reality—in my own life as well as in others'—is that sometimes when I take a day away, I'm simply drowning in things and exhausted. So having the energy even to think about the future—or options or the big picture—isn't possible. I find myself just sitting. Finally there's silence!—no phones, no demands, no unsolvable—or at least unsolved—problems to face.

Ulrich Zwingli

Almighty, eternal, and merciful God, whose Word is a lamp unto our feet and a light unto our path, open and illuminate our minds, that we may purely and perfectly understand thy Word and that our lives may be conformed to what we have rightly understood, that in nothing we may be displeasing to thy majesty, through Jesus Christ our Lord. Amen.

–the prayer with which Zwingli began his Bible lectures in Zurich each day

It's important, then, to give yourself a little time to rebuild your energy level. To help you do that, the first thing to do when you get away is to take a blank sheet of paper and write down all the things you have to do when you get home. Just dump them out of your system. Empty yourself.

Then keep that pad of paper handy, and every time you think, *Well, I should call Mrs. Smith* or *I should call Mr. Jones*, write it down. It lets your mind stay focused on the future.

Next, rest for a while. The average pastor works 50 hours a week; many work 60 to 80 hours a week and get calls in the middle of the night. So spend an hour or two just resting your system—looking at the sky, looking at the mountains, looking at the trees. Watch them and thank God for them. Get back in touch with who God is. Rest your emotions and your mind. Only then can you begin to ask questions about the future.

The 10 Key Questions

1. *What is my single greatest strength?*

A few years ago, I went through what I call a "midlife reevaluation." The question that pulled me out of that more than any other was this: "What is my single greatest strength?" It focused my thoughts.

When you're wondering whether you should stay in the pastorate, move to a different church, start counseling more, or make some other major change, and the fog sets in regarding who you are, ask yourself, "What is my single greatest strength? What do I do best?"

When I ask pastors to answer that question about themselves, a lot of them say, "My single greatest strength is my integrity."

I reply, "Yes, that's your 'B-Side' strength, your flip-side strength. But what do you do best?"

Often they will respond, "Well, I'm a pastor."

I have to say, "Yes, but why are you a good pastor? What's the single thing you really do well?"

Once you get that strength in focus, you're going to find that it becomes the basis on which you can make a lot of decisions about things you shouldn't be doing, because they aren't really things you do well.

Sometimes, of course, you have to do everything just because it's "there." Churchill said, "Sometimes our best isn't enough; we have to do what is required." In a small-church pastorate, that's understandable. But you still want to ask yourself, "What is my single greatest strength—my greatest talent, my greatest gift? And how do I maximize that?"

Answering this question is one of the best uses of time you can make. It's where you have the most stewardship responsibility for your life. The good can be the enemy of the best, and often we settle for "just stuff" and do not give ourselves to the thing we do best.

One caveat here is that the average pastor will respond, "Well, I do a lot of things better than most people I know." That can sound arrogant, but it's not. It's just a reality. Many pastors are bright people. They speak and think better than most people they know. So a lot of pastors have never taken the time or discipline to define their answer to this question. I encourage you to nail down your answer.

On the other hand, you may be inclined to say there's nothing you do really well. Statistics from a recent survey show that 70 percent of ministers say their self-image is lower now than it was when they began pastoring. But a lot of people don't understand what self-image—or self-concept—really is. By my definition, it's this: Self-concept is the sum total of all the adjectives you use to describe yourself. So if you say, "I don't know who I am," "I'm in this midlife reevaluation," or "I'm just a new pastor—I'm 25 years old," get a piece of paper and make an exhaustive list of every adjective you would use to describe yourself, positive and negative. That's your self-concept.

The person who says, "My self-image is lower than it used to be," means he's using a larger number of negative adjectives like *overwhelmed, incompetent*, and so on instead of *confident* and *productive*.

A lot of times, your list needs objective evaluation from a mentor, professor, wife, close friend, or your church board. You may think you're incompetent, whereas everybody around you is saying, "No, he's one of the most competent people I've ever met!"

I also suggest you read through the New Testament sometime, making a list of all the adjectives God used as He described you.

Be careful, too, not to compare yourself with other pastors. If you do, it's easy to go home and say, "What is this paltry thing I'm trying to do here?" But the fact is that you're not Chuck Swindoll or R. C. Sproul. You don't have their strengths or calling. You're not me, and I'm not you. You need to define who you are, what strengths God has given you, and what He expects of you. We need Chuck Swindoll and R. C. Sproul, but we also need me and you.

The clearer you can be on who you are, what your strengths are, what you're doing, and the rightness of that calling, the less comparison you'll need.

2. *What three decisions are causing me the greatest stress?*

Talking with a publisher the other day, I said, "What are the things you're seeing that you want to see more books written about, because those things are just everywhere?"

He replied, "Stress. Stress is everywhere."

I recently calculated that I had spent roughly 21,000 hours in the last 16 years behind the defenses of Christian executives, pastors, Christian leaders, and Christian businesspeople, and I've seen stress in every one of them at one level or another. Scripture's "Be anxious for nothing" seems to have escaped their attention! They're saying, "I don't know how to deal with it."

In talking with those leaders, I've found two main causes of stress. The first is indecision, and the second is lack of control. Eighty percent of the time when stress is a problem, we can drastically reduce it by finding answers to one or both of these questions: (1) "What are the three decisions you're trying to make that you just can't make?" (2) "What's out of control?"

A true leader is someone who knows (1) what to do next, (2) why that's important, and (3) how to bring the appropriate resources to bear on the need at hand. Whoever doesn't know those things begins to falter as a leader regardless of his title.

3. *What is overwhelming me?*

When someone I'm consulting with is feeling overwhelmed, I make this suggestion: "Get a blank sheet of paper and a pencil, and for the next 10 minutes, write out your answer to this question: What's heavy on my shoulders today?" I have the person make an exhaustive list; it might include calls he has to make, a gift he has to buy, something he has to check on, something he has to find an answer to, or any number of other things.

When I have pastors do this, they sometimes come back with a list of 70 or more things! They will be items of the "I should do this" variety.

It's extremely helpful, however, to get all those confettilike pieces out of your brain and onto paper so you can begin to say, "All right, which of these do I have to do today? Which could I postpone until next week? Next month? Next year?" Another tack is to ask, "What are the three nonnegotiables I have to get done today?" or some other similar question that will get you to process the list.

Get it out of your head, off your heart, and onto paper so you can see it and deal with it.

Here's the logic of writing down such a list. Let's say that your wife asks you to go to the supermarket and pick up 10 things. You could try to memorize that list, keep it clear in your head, and not forget anything before you get to the store. But as you drive, your mind thinks about nothing other than those 10 items. You go over them and over them. You can't concentrate on other things.

But if you get that list down on a piece of paper, you can put it in your pocket and think about whatever else you want all the time until you get to the store. You've dealt with it. You don't have the anxiety or the guilt. You don't have to worry, *Have I forgotten something?*

The same is true for the list that comes to your mind in answer to the question, "What's overwhelming me?" Just get it onto paper.

4. *What impassable roadblock has me stuck?*

More specifically, this question can be, "In all my work, what is the single thing which, if I could just solve it, would allow everything else to just flow?"

Typically, the answer is "money" or "people." But many times, there are other answers as well: "We don't have the right church building" or "We don't have the right this or whatever." But this is one of the most clarifying questions to answer, because it sometimes seems as if the answer is "Everything is holding me back! I don't have money; I don't have people; I don't have ideas; I don't have a church; I don't have buildings; I don't have . . ." The list can go on and on.

My response, though, is, "But what's the one thing that's holding back everything else?" Once you identify that, it's much easier to get your board working with you to solve that problem. Your board will also respond much better to 1 challenge than to 50.

5. *If I could do only three things in my lifetime, what would they be?*

This is the second question that really helped to clear my mind when I did my midlife reevaluation. It can also be nuanced in this way: "What are either the three goals you'd like to reach before you die or the three problems you'd like to solve or be part of solving before you die?"

Most people in America, including pastors, think seasonally. They think, *What are we going to do between now and Christmas?* Their year focuses on Christmas, the missions conference, Easter, vacation Bible school, the opening of Sunday school, and so on. They find it hard to think in terms of an annual plan. To think in terms of the year 2000, 2010, and so on is even more difficult.

I've found, though, that this question #5 is actually easier than any of the 3-, 5-, or 10-year questions. Most people's minds lock into what they want to do before they die. But your answers to this question have to be in measurable terms. And once you answer this question, you clarify for yourself what to do at a whole lot of places where your road forks in two or more different directions. Yogi Berra said, "When you come to a fork in the road, take it!" With this question answered, you can do just that, because you'll know what to do and what not to do.

6. *What should I resign from or drop out of?*

Once you've answered the questions "What is my single greatest strength?" and "What are the three things I'd like to do before I die?" so that you have a better focus on your life, then it's much easier to say, "Hey, wait a minute! This committee I'm on really has nothing to do with anything."

A lot of people ask me, "Bobb, are you into time management?" I say, "No." They then say, "What do you mean?" And I say, "Well, Scripture's view of time management is, 'One day time shall be no more.'" In one sense, time is an insignificant nothing in Scripture. So significance and making a difference for eternity and all those kinds of things are important to me, but saving 5 or 10 minutes here and there isn't really what I'm about.

What I *am* about is being effective. "Efficiency is doing things right," Peter Drucker says, "and effectiveness is doing right things." I'd much rather help a man decide what *not* to do—which will save him 2 days a year, or 20 or even 50. I've had people say to me, "Bobb, with this clarification, I'm going to resign this board, and it will save me 7 days a year." That's a lot of 5 and 10 minutes here and there!

So what I'm after is, what are the fundamental right things for you to be doing in relationship to the giftedness you've been given, your God-given dreams, and so on? And then, what can you stop doing? You take the time you save and spend it with your family or use it for doing the things God has called and gifted you to do.

7. *What can I postpone—be it for a month, three months, or indefinitely?*

A man met a pastor, and almost immediately the pastor was telling him every committee he was on, how he was chairman of hospital boards and civic organizations. He was also a father and, of course, a pastor. It was exhausting just to hear the list, and the one thought that came to the listener's mind was, *How long is it going to be before he just explodes or drops something that's really significant—or loses his church because his people say, "He's not pastoring; he's being a civic leader. We need a pastor"?*

Your board can often give you profound wisdom when it comes to answering this question. But I don't necessarily mean your official board—the elders, directors, or vestry. I'm talking about an advisory council of people you really respect. Give them a list of the things you're involved in and say, "What would you encourage me to reconsider?"

Chuck Colson is a good example. He brings himself into an accountability position with people in whom he has great confidence—so much so that he allows them to help structure his schedule. For a lot of us, having someone to help us set our schedule and then ask us big questions about the time we're giving to family, devotions, and so forth will make a major difference.

8. *What things on my to-do list can someone else do at least 80 percent as well?*

This question has been a real fog cutter for a lot of people who find it difficult to delegate. If someone else can do something 80 percent as well as you, you'd better let him do it. If he can do it only 10 percent as well, don't let him have it yet.

Many pastors I work with would say something like, "I am terribly limited in life because I'm not in a big-enough church to afford a paid staff." I tell them this story: One night I was flying from Salt Lake City into Orange County, where I lived in California. I sat next to a distinguished-looking man. It turned out that he was one of the attorneys for the Mormons. We got to talking, and I asked him, "How many members do you have in the United States?" He said about three million, as I recall. I also asked, "Well, how many paid staff do you have?" Now, stop for a minute and make your own guess about how many paid staff they have.

Some people guess 300,000 people on paid staff. Others guess 30,000—and so on. But, according to this man, they have 12 paid staff in their entire organization in the United States—the elders in Salt Lake City. All the local people are volunteers working a paid job outside the church, including the man who is the equivalent of the senior pastor in an evangelical church.

The point is, you can get a lot done with volunteers. I'd like to encourage you in this matter. There may be many laymen in your church who could have been good senior pastors; they just chose to go to IBM or to work for themselves instead of to seminary. Begin to see those people as full-time people (full-time staff people) who can work in the church only 10 (or 5 or whatever) hours a week.

Here's an interesting and fun way to find those people. Stand up some Sunday morning and say, "If any of you would someday like to be in full-time Christian service (10 or 20 years from now, or maybe when you retire), I'd like to invite you to coffee tomorrow night at my house." And then just see who shows up! You might find that some of the people you think would never leave business are thinking of going into full-time service someday.

Then on Monday night you say, "Now, to get you ready for that future Christian service, let's make sure you get a wide variety of work assignments. Why don't you be the volunteer director of Christian education this year, the volunteer director of the counseling center next year, and the church administrator the next year?" You get this high-powered volunteer working through the paces so that when the application comes from a seminary, a mission board, or another church that says, "We're considering this person," you can say, "He's worked here for seven years and has done everything with excellence," as compared to, "He hasn't tried anything here, and he's just been rusting in the pew. I didn't realize he was interested!"

That one idea could find the two, three, or four people who could be some of your core team for the next few years in the church. And these are the people you give the things that they can do 80 percent as well as you can.

Also—and this is something you can do even if you're in a small church—take someone with you when you go calling at hospitals and nursing homes. You'll enjoy the person's company, and it'll let that person see what ministerial life is all about. Then, when those times come up when you're unable to do something, you'll have these friends—who didn't even realize they were in training—who are equipped to go and do exactly what they saw you doing.

9. *What are the elephants in my schedule?*

Italian economist Vilfredo Pareto said, "If you're Noah, and your ark is about to sink, look for the elephants first, because you can throw over a bunch of cats and dogs and squirrels and everything else that is just a small animal—and your ark will keep sinking. But if you can find one elephant to get overboard, you're in much better shape."

Now, Pareto used this illustration in relation to budgets. You can find an item in your budget that's maybe 1 percent of your budget, spend 10 hours working on that item, and figure out how to save 50 percent—but you'll save only pennies. If, on the other hand, you can find the thing that's costing you 50 percent of your budget and then save 10 percent on that item, you'll save a whole lot more money.

The same logic holds with schedules. As I said earlier, what things are taking 7 days out of your year? If you can arrive at just 1 major decision such as, "I'm going to resign from this particular board or this particular assignment"—boom!—it gets 7 days out of your scheduled time, or even a month. If you save just 10 or 20 minutes here and there, it really doesn't make any difference. Get rid of those elephants first.

10. *What three things could I do in the next three months that would make a 50 percent difference?*

This is a question that Steve Douglass, executive vice president of

Campus Crusade for Christ, taught me. It is one of the best questions I've heard because it prioritizes at three levels.

The bottom-line essence of it is this: Consider your biggest project. Maybe it's erecting a church building or hiring a staff person. And simply ask yourself, What 3 things could we do in the next 90 days to make a 50 percent difference?

Steve Douglass went on to say, "What most people do is ask, 'What are the 300 things we could do in the next 9 years to get us 100 percent of the way there?'" He concluded, "I want the big chunks first." What that does is to separate the dust from the boulders, the pebbles from the stones. It gives you a fundamental big picture on almost any assignment you have. For example, "What 3 things could our church do in the next 90 days to make a 50 percent difference? What 3 things could the Christian education department do in the next 90 days to make a 50 percent difference?"

One of the things I find leaders often aren't sure of when they bring in a layman as a volunteer or a new staff member is the kind of assignments to give the person. I say to these leaders, "If I took over your staff at your church today, the first thing I would do is try to establish a trust relationship with those people. But the second thing I would do is make sure they had a crystal-clear understanding of the 3 goals they were to reach or the 3 problems they were to solve in the next 90 days. Once they have that understanding, they have a clear track to run, and they are free to begin working toward getting those things done. This is all fundamental to building a team." So ask of yourself, of each staff member, of your board, of the whole church, of the committee you serve on, "What 3 things could each person do in the next 90 days to make a 50 percent difference by the year 2000 or 2010?"

Sometimes, to set goals is to solve problems. And sometimes goals and problems are the same thing, essentially. But often the reality is that problems are within the existing system, whereas goals are typically outside the system and new to it. It doesn't matter, however, whether you're dealing with goals or problems. If you like setting goals, go ahead and set goals. If you like solving problems, go ahead and solve them. What you're after in either case is focus, which leads to results. You want to make sure your team has a clear focus for the next 90 days.

Two Additional Questions for Young Pastors

I have two additional questions for young pastors—questions that get at the heart of a pastor's life.

1. *What is your passion?*
2. *What is your dream?*

Those two questions sound alike, but they're very different. "What is your passion?" means "What do you feel deeply burdened by and uniquely qualified to deal with today? What are you really emotional about?" But "What is your dream?" means "What is your long-term plan? Where do you eventually want to be or go or do?"

Those two questions are good for clarification. So as part of your retreat day, and in addition to the 10 preceding questions, ask yourself, "Pastor, what is your passion at this point?" Some people will say, "Well, it's the abortion issue." Others will say, "It's teenagers," "It's the drug problem," or it may be prison work or church growth.

A dream, on the other hand, is what life would be like if the needs you see were actually met. In other words, if your need is a new staff, new buildings, more capital, new vans, or whatever else, and if all those needs were met, what would life be like? That's your dream; that's your vision.

A lot of pastors say, "I'm not a visionary, Bobb, but people expect me to be a visionary." I respond, "Let me clarify what a visionary is. A visionary is simply a person who looks into the future, sees what the needs are, and can paint a word picture of what life would be like if those needs were met." To be a visionary is to be able to say, "We're going to build this building, and here's what life will be like in the new building."

A Word of Hope

Too many people have no dreams. It's heartbreaking to see well-trained, wonderful, loving pastors whom God has called and ordained living lives of nothingness, with no passion, no dreams, and no ability to get up and get going again. All their dreams have been beaten down.

Then there are those people who have never dreamed a lot. They didn't dream before they went into the pastorate, and they don't dream now. And that's okay. You can accomplish much for God and not be a dreamer or a visionary. You need to ask yourself at a gut level—when no one else is watching or listening—"Am I a goal-setter, or am I a problem-solver?" The goal-setters tend to be dreamers, and the problem-solvers tend to be practical, to get in the trenches and make things happen.

Either way, I want to leave you with three principles.

Principle 1: One way or another, you have to build a team or you're going to drown in all the stuff you have to do. You just can't do it all yourself.

Principle 2: You have to schedule time away. Jesus scheduled time away. When He fed the five thousand and healed some of the sick, He could have set up a counseling line or even a healing line that day and stayed there the rest of His life. But what did He do? He got away. He went out onto the lake. At other times, He went into the desert or into the mountains.

Pastor, I don't care how far behind you are. At some point you have to say, "I am going to take a day away. I'm going to take that retreat. No matter what happens in the church, I'm going to take a day away with my wife." You have to schedule it or it never happens, because there's never a "good" time to get away.

Principle 3: You must see that what you are doing in terms of balance in your life is a model for a lot of your laymen. Are they seeing a model that says, "A real Christian never takes a day off, works 70 or 80 hours a week, and is overwhelmed by things all the time"? What you ought to model for your board of directors, your elders, your vestry, and your laymen is that a Christian leader can take time away with his family. In fact, a Christian leader *needs* to take time away for refreshment. Real Christian people get away. They build teams, and they take time off.

Don't feel, however, that you have to be a perfectly balanced person. You'll never get there! So decide this day, "I will never be a perfectly balanced person; I'll just keep working toward it. Whenever I get out of balance, I'll get away, dump my to-do list, rest a bit, ask the questions in this chapter, and refocus my future." That's not only following what Jesus did, but it also provides a healthy model for the church.

Pastor *to* Pastor

The word balance *is probably as important as any in the English language, because the opposite of being balanced is to be eccentric. When you're out of balance, things wear out. Tires go bald, machines break, nerves are on edge, and the list goes on and on.*

Jesus was a great example of One who lived a balanced life. He knew how to balance crisis management with rest and recreation; conversation with friends and family with intense confrontation with those who sought to call Him into account. Jesus was also wise enough to get away to a distant place where He could recoup, gather His thoughts, and prepare for the next step.

I haven't always practiced balance in my life. I lived eccentrically during a lot of my 31 years in the pastorate. I wish I could have some of that time back—time for my kids and for Beverley. God has been merciful to restore many of the years the locusts had eaten, but the sad thing is that He shouldn't have had to, because a lot of it was my fault. I insisted on keeping a schedule that was much too complicated, because I thought in many ways that I could fix everything. Also, probably because of my insecurity, I felt I had to have the answers to every question anyone asked. As I look back over that time, I realize I was mistaken all around.

If I have anything to say to you as a mentor, as a "pastor to pastor," as one who has probably walked in your shoes somewhere along the journey, it would be to take Bobb Biehl's advice and get away for a little while. Take a pencil and a piece of paper, and begin asking—and answering—those big questions.

H. B. L.

8

In several of the preceding chapters, we have touched in one way or another on the issue of success in ministry. What is it? How do we attain it?

I sincerely believe this chapter is one of the most valuable in our book. The reason: It comes from the heart of a pastor who tasted failure, as man might perceive it, before he came to understand the real meaning of success.

When the edition of "Pastor to Pastor" called "Shepherding, Servanthood and Success" hit the pastors' mailboxes, the response, as we imagined it might be, was very encouraging. Let me share with you how some of our clergy friends responded.

"As pastor of one of those small churches that make up the majority of Christianity, I'm deeply encouraged by the attitude of this volume. . . . It's great to hear a seasoned veteran encourage us to keep on pressing on rather than hear another message on how we're doing it all wrong and need to build up a 'mega church' to be considered a success in ministry."

On another note, a pastor wrote, "It seems to me that we as clergy are too wrapped up in the 'success syndrome,' which drives us into competition with other clergy outside our denominations, clergy within our own denominations, and even with ourselves."

And from a couple whose ministry is encouraging pastors, "Many of the 'Pastor to Pastor' editions are valuable resources, but the most helpful has been the one entitled 'Shepherding, Servanthood and Success.' The tapes really help stress revival and reach many pastors who are at the threshold of giving up."

I remember a time I was allowed the privilege of ministry to a group of missionaries stationed in Japan. Many of them had gone years between converts. They had labored, prayed, sacrificed, and probably even questioned their value to the cause of Christ. But you will read in this chapter Kent Hughes's words that say, "God sees things in a much different way from the way the world sees things. He's looking for people who are faithful to His Word and are hard-

working where He has placed them." Amen. Bloom where you're planted, my friend. You do your part, God will do His, and when the battle is over, we'll divide up the spoils of victory. And we will be victorious—that's a promise!

H. B. London Jr.

Slaying the Success Syndrome

by Kent Hughes

Anyone who deals with pastors knows a lot of them who are doing everything right, but they still don't feel successful, and others who are feeling on top of the world but who might need to re-examine their priorities.

My Failure

At one point, I had all the things that nearly any of us would like for the ministry—support to begin a new church, demographic studies, and seed money—a trailer full of all the things necessary to set up a church. But those weren't the things needed for success in ministry.

Let me tell you about that time—a time of huge failure in my life.

I was converted at age 12, and I had typical youthful expectations. It was during the mid-1950s, and I looked up to Billy Graham. So after I was converted, I just assumed I was going to be the next Billy Graham! That's how I looked at success then, which is acceptable in a 12-year-old.

When I got into my teenage years, I was focused because of my commitment to Jesus. I preached my first sermon at 16. In college, I preached on the streets of Los Angeles. That's also when I met Barbara. She's a real soul-winner who has the joy of life, so marrying her, with all her qualities, just confirmed my great expectations for myself. I began in the ministry with 10 years of youth work in the 1960s. Those were difficult years in some ways, but they were also a time of huge harvests for the kingdom of God.

At the end of the 1960s, I decided to get off on my own and begin a church. That's the time mentioned above when, according to man's estimation of things, I had everything going for me: youth, education, past evidences of ability, a supportive wife, a nucleus of 20 families—not to mention a $50,000 gift from a sponsoring church. We headed into a Southern California targeted community with supposedly everything we needed. How could I miss? Before we went out to start the new church, everyone told me that as a "fair-haired boy," I would soon have the daughter church growing bigger than the parent church.

And I believed all those things.

Well, we did it "right." We did the demographic surveys, aerial photographs, and so on. But after a couple of years of intense work, we had fewer people than we had had in the first six months!

Consequently, I entered into a dark and deep depression. I questioned God's goodness. That experience wasn't the hardest thing I've gone through in the ministry, but it was bad enough that it almost made me quit. It forced a real crisis in my life—and in Barbara's.

Everything came to a head one night when I was extremely depressed, and I poured out my heart to Barbara: all my frustrations about the way things were as opposed to my thinking about what "success in the ministry" means. But I had imbibed a totally secular way of thinking about success. And at the end of our conversation, I found myself coming to a conclusion that I didn't want to admit. But it had been brewing in me for so long that finally it just bubbled to the surface, and I said, "God has called me to do something He has not given me the gift to accomplish. Therefore, God is not good."

Barbara was sitting there, listening to me say that (and all the broodings that led up to it), and she realized I was in deep trouble. Think about it: Here I was in the ministry of spiritual service to others, but I had come to the conclusion that God isn't good!

When I realized what I had said, I asked, "Oh Barbara, what am I going to do?"

She said, "Kent, I don't know what you're going to do about all of it. But for tonight—just for tonight—hang on to my faith, because I believe. I believe God is good, that He loves us, and that He's going to see us through this. So hang on to my faith; I have enough for both of us."

I had been pouring my heart out to her for an hour or so. I was exhausted, frustrated, and spent. So after she said that, I just sighed deeply and went off to bed. Barbara had extended her faith to me, so I was able to relax.

But Barbara couldn't sleep. She was perplexed and shaken. She went into the kitchen, sat down, and felt afraid. Here she had extended her faith to me, but as she reflected on all I had said, she thought, *Well, do I have enough faith for us both? Is my faith strong? Is God really there?*

In response, she wanted to do what she's always done when she's afraid: She wanted to read her Bible.

But the Bible she always read was in the bedroom with me. Not wanting to disturb me, she took off the shelf a Bible that had been given to her a year before. It was in the kitchen with her cookbooks, and it had never been used that she could recall. It was so new that the pages were still stuck together!

She sat down and prayed to God, saying, "Lord, I need a word from You right now. I've never done this before, but I need a word. If You're really there and You care about what's happening to us (and I believe You

Steve Farrar

We live in Little Rock, Arkansas. Before that, we lived in California, where land and housing are pretty expensive. The lots tend to be small there. So, in California we had a small backyard, and I had a little push mower. Well, we moved to Little Rock, and suddenly I had a backyard a third of an acre in size.

The first day I mowed the grass was in August. The temperature was over 100 degrees, and the humidity was over 90 percent. It took me 8 hours and 22 bags of clippings, and I'm not exaggerating!

When I was done, I had a real sense of contentment. Our house was about 10 years old, it had a fresh coat of white paint, and, seen amid the manicured, green grass, it looked great!

After that hard day's work, I went inside to get some iced tea and sit down. I was just flipping through a magazine to relax, and I saw this article about this couple in Des Moines who had redone their kitchen. It had all the before-and-after pictures. It was quite a transformation: from old,

are and do), and if You really can, will You please give me a word of encouragement?"

Then she did what we don't recommend that people do. She played Bible roulette! She opened her Bible at random and stuck her finger down on a page. And there on the page was a verse underlined in red, which caught her eye. She has no idea how that verse came to be underlined; it was the only such verse in that whole new Bible. Actually, she says, "I just 'happened' to open to that page by God's direction, I'm sure."

So she said, "Okay, Lord, I'm going to read that verse"—and it was as if everything hinged on God's speaking to her in that moment.

This is what she read: "Though he fall, he shall not be utterly cast down: for the LORD upholdeth him with his hand" (Ps. 37:24, KJV).

As Barbara puts it, "It was so awesome to me. It was as if the sovereign God was in my little kitchen. He spoke to me. He met me in my moment of need. The verse just previous said, 'The steps of a good man are ordered by the LORD: and he delighteth in his way.' Then comes, 'Though he fall, he shall not be utterly cast down.' It was just what I needed. The Lord met me. All my fear dissipated. I felt that 'Yes, there's a God in heaven; He hears; He knows; He's sovereignly in control.' I was able to go to bed and fall asleep next to Kent reciting that promise—Though he fall, he won't be utterly cast down."

The next morning came, and Barbara told

me what had happened. Through that and some other events that occurred that week, I repented, and we covenanted that we would be thoroughly biblical in seeking out what success is. So in the next months, we did just that, and the things we learned began to formulate our understanding of what success is biblically. That, in turn, started to work our liberation from the success syndrome.

Success and . . . the Numbers

Humanly speaking, there is among pastors an insatiable desire to be successful. And so often, success is couched in the terms of bottom lines—how many, how much, how often. Consequently, we have many pastors who would give anything if their churches would grow at all. (The statistics say that right now, two-thirds of all the churches in America are either in decline or on a plateau.)

Every place you look, we're closing churches. So whatever success is, if it's growth in numbers, there aren't many pastors who are having it. Yet it's easy to see success in just those terms. For one thing, we just naturally want to see numbers. Also, we have to deal with the external pressures we get from our secular culture, which puts a number value on everything. And then there's the very God-given desire for souls. So the link between success and numbers is undeniable.

I admit that I look at the numbers from our church every Monday morning, and I'm

stained Formica countertops to beautiful ceramic tile, from hardly any cupboard space to French doors with a rotating pantry. I flipped the page, and there was another article about a couple in Boise who had redone their back deck, and it was incredible. It followed the contour of the land and had a barbecue area. (I think they even had an amphitheatre there. It was just amazing.)

Anyway, I was out of tea at that point. I went into our kitchen to get more, and as I walked in, I stopped cold and looked at our kitchen—the countertops, made of Formica. I went to the pantry to get some Sweet 'n Low; it didn't rotate. There weren't French doors.

Suddenly, I wasn't pleased with our kitchen. I thought, *Why do we live in a roach trap like this anyway?* I looked out at my deck, which I'd enjoyed all day, and I thought, *You know, I've seen firewood in better shape than that deck.* In about a seven-minute period, I went from a state of contentment to being discontent.

Interestingly, it was all from reading a magazine. As I looked at better kitchens and better decks, suddenly I was discontent with what I had. It was amazing how quickly the transformation took place.

Years ago, I heard Howard Hendricks say that comparison is the favorite indoor sport of Christians. And I think he was right. Whether I compare my ministry, my house, or my car to someone else's—it's just endless. There's always something better than what we have. Influenza used to kill people; now we have to deal with affluenza.

Comparison kills contentment. That's the issue. And it's an issue we pastors deal with daily in so many areas of our lives.

affected by whether they're down or up. But I also know those numbers don't indicate success or its lack. Now, I'm not saying numbers aren't important. The Bible tells us Jesus fed 5,000 and 3,000 were saved at Pentecost. But I also understand that if the Lord was in it and He was presiding over it and only 5 had been fed and only 3 had been saved at Pentecost, it would have been a great success anyway. God sees things much differently from the way we do. So I'm not knocking numbers, but I am saying that whether you're on their up side or their down side, you'd better have a biblical definition of success—because your soul can be in the balance.

But when we as pastors don't see those increasing numbers, we think, *I'm not a success*. That's exactly what happened to me in the story I told above. And in the deepest, darkest depression of my life, I poured my heart out to my wife. And then we resolved to find out what the Bible has to say about success. Consequently, we've found that there is a better definition of success than having more people the next Sunday than you had the last Sunday.

Biblical Success

I'm invited to speak at conferences, and one reason is that I pastor a large church. But because of our earlier experience, when Barbara and I came to College Church and it began to grow, it meant much less to us than a lot of people think. We understood that I could pastor a large church and still not hear from Him (when I stand before Him), "Well done, thou good and faithful servant."

What, then, is success according to the Scriptures?

1. First, success is faithfulness that shows itself in obedience to God's Word. We discovered that nowhere in Scripture does it say that we're called to be successful per se. Success will be mentioned as a result of something, but it doesn't say we're called to be successful. We did find a passage, however, that says stewards are required to be faithful (see 1 Cor. 4:1-2). So I understood that if I was going to have any success in God's eyes, it had to be rooted in faithfulness. Then I began to think about the concept of faithfulness.

There's a wonderful story in Numbers 20 where the people of Israel, after the 40 years of wilderness wandering, were rebelling against Moses because they wanted water and food. They had done that 40 years earlier, when God had told Moses to smite the rock and produce water. This time, God said, "I want you to speak to the rock." And Moses, in his great agony of soul and his anger at his people, instead struck it twice. Water poured out of the rock, and all Israel was supplied.

Moses was the great hero of the day, because he gave the people exactly what they wanted. But that's earth's point of view. From heaven's perspective, it was the day of Moses' greatest failure. Because he didn't honor God as holy and obey His word, Moses didn't enter the Promised Land. He didn't get his heart's desire, even though he appeared to be immensely successful to the people.

Barbara and I came to understand that you can be heralded as successful—people can be singing your accolades; you can be giving them the Word; your church can be growing—but from heaven's point of view, you're not a success because you're not being faithful to God and His Word. So we understood that success is rooted in profound obedience to the Lord and the Bible.

What's great about the idea of success as faithfulness is that anybody can be faithful! You don't have to be gifted or talented. No matter what your limitations, you can be faithful to what God has called you to do. Of course, as pastors, that's to preach the Word, give the gospel, and disciple people—all the things Scripture tells us to do.

Success, then, is immensely egalitarian. It's available to everybody. We knew that we could be faithful, and you can, too.

The reason that under God's sovereign hand there has recently been such a harvest of souls in Africa and South America is that for generations, people went there and plugged away in faithful ministry with few converts. They were the planters. And now is the time of harvest.

2. *Second, though, faithfulness is not a cop-out for lethargy, apathy, or faintness of heart.* Success is hardworking. This ingredient of faithfulness (and of success) is clearly laid out in Matthew 25, the parable of the talents. One servant is given one talent, another is given two talents, and the third is given five talents. The two-talent and five-talent people go do something with what they've been given, but the person who's been given the one talent buries it. The lord comes back, and he says to the ones who did something with their talents, "Well done, thou good and faithful servant." But the lord condemns the one who didn't do anything as a wicked, lazy (slothful) servant.

The parable juxtaposes sloth and faith. You cannot be a lazy, faithful servant! Faithfulness has to be hardworking; it has to be creative; but God is the one who gives the increase.

3. *Third, there is no success apart from a foot-washing heart.* The faithful minister will have a servant's attitude. Jesus said, "Now that I, your Lord and Teacher, have washed your feet, you also should wash one another's feet" (John 13:14). We can be in megachurches and not have a servant's heart. If you want to test whether you have a servant's heart, see how you feel the next time someone treats you like a servant.

4. *Fourth, there is no success apart from loving God with all that we have and are.* The great shema of the Old Testament says, "Hear, O Israel: The LORD our God, the LORD is one. Love the LORD your God with all your

heart and with all your soul and with all your strength" (Deut. 6:4-5). And then you find Jesus quoting the shema when He was asked by a lawyer which is the greatest commandment in the law (see Matt. 22:34-40). And there is Peter's reinstatement when Jesus asked if he loved Him (see John 21:15-17).

So we understand that you could pastor a huge church and not love God with all your heart. You could write a book on loving God and not love Him with all your heart. All these things could be cold ashes on the altar if we really don't love Him.

5. *Fifth, success must contain faith.* Hebrews 11:6 says that without faith, it is impossible to please God, because you must believe that He exists and rewards those who diligently seek Him. So Barbara and I realized that in order to have success, we need to be believing people.

In my dark night of the soul that I described earlier, I wasn't believing what I actually knew and defended. In an important sense, then, we need to believe what we believe. We need to put our trust in the fact that the basic things we say we believe are, indeed, true.

6. *Sixth, success comes to people of prayer.* The average pastor spends so little time in prayer. Malachi 2:6 says, "True instruction was in his mouth and nothing false was found on his lips. He walked with me in peace and uprightness, and turned many from sin."

"Of all men," wrote Horatius Bonar, "a minister of Christ is especially called to walk with God. Everything depends on this; his own peace and joy, his own future reward at the coming of the Lord. But especially does God point to this as the true and sure way of securing blessing. This is the grand secret of ministerial success. One who walks with God reflects the light of His countenance upon a benighted world; and the closer he walks, the more of this light does he reflect." This leads into the seventh element of success: holiness.

7. *Seventh, to be successful, we must be holy*. Leviticus 19:2 says that we're to be holy because God is holy. That refers to all the believing

people. Exodus 28:36-37, though, says that the Old Testament priest was to have on his turban a gold plate, and on that plate were to be engraved these words: "Holy to the Lord." In the New Testament, Peter called the whole church to be holy (see 1 Pet. 1:13-16; 2:5, 9), and Paul said elders must be "self-controlled, upright, holy and disciplined" (Titus 1:8).

We hear week after week about pastors who fall into sexual immorality. If we're not holy, we can't call ourselves a success, regardless of what's going on with our church's attendance figures.

Howard Hendricks made the statement that (at some point in time) there have been 150-160 pastors of large churches who have fallen into moral failure. And that means, for one thing, that thousands of people were looking up to those pastors, thinking they were the pinnacle of success, when in God's eyes they were abysmal failures. Os Guinness said, "You can build a church without God if you want to." And what's sad is that those pastors think they're successful.

You can build up a Wallstrum's Wonder, where you've got everything in place and you press the button and all the gears move, but there's no presence of the Holy Spirit. It's just that you have figured out, from a sociological and managerial point of view, how to create an engine that runs. Pragmatism, if it's carried to the nth degree, will corrupt your theology. The attitude of "If it works, do it" is foreign to biblical principles of life and success. The true picture of the church is what it stands for, its teaching and beliefs.

The Daughter and the Son

Pastors often go to convention after convention, and Christians spend millions and millions of dollars on the church-growth movement. The people who sit on the platforms and do the speaking are those who have the biggest attendance numbers, the largest sanctuaries, and the greatest numbers of baptisms. But all those other pastors serve in the little hamlets and the dying communities: the pastors whose churches have a difficult time growing because the population of the community shrinks 3 or 4 percent a year. Those pastors sit back there and feel, in many ways, that they're insignificant, that they don't matter, that they could drop off the edge of the world and nobody would even know. At times, they wonder why they're doing what they're doing. Life can be dark and dismal for them. When they think of the word *success* as it's commonly used, they would say it's the last word that would describe them.

So in addition to what I've written above, I encourage you who feel that way to turn your minds again to an understanding that God is the Father. He's not the president of IBM. He doesn't look at things the same way we do. I would also point out the apostle Paul's words, "As for those who seemed to be important . . . those men added nothing to my message" (Gal. 2:6)!

God is looking for people who are faithful to His Word and are hard-working where He has placed them. If that's the principle we apply, we can say that people who are ministering in the Muslim world today—where they may not see even one convert in their lifetime—are by no means failures. All of us have to be faithful in the culture and place where God has put us. That's how God measures success.

It's true that every week, a church in the United States moves beyond the 1,000-member level. At the same time, though, 8 out of 10 seminary graduates will never serve a church with more than 150 people in it. But whether you're on the up side or the down side of the numbers, you need a biblical definition of success. In fact, a man's ministry and soul can be in danger when he's on the up side of the numbers if he's not operating under that definition. But if he is, it's very liberating. Then, in a sense, the numbers don't matter; it's the faithfulness that counts.

Several months after Barbara and I had begun to study the Scriptures and, for our own well-being, had arrived at a new definition of success, I had a whole new attitude. Even though we had few people (25 on a Sunday night) when I got up to preach, I was different because my focus was different.

What really cemented it for us, though, was something we realized when our children were in the Christmas play at school. Our eldest daughter, Holly, had the lead in O. Henry's "The Gift of the Magi." She was Della, the woman who has her hair cut off in order to sell it and buy her husband a watch fob. So Holly was a lovely Victorian heroine, and she (if I may say so) charmed the whole audience. She had her lines down pat. At the end of the performance, everyone just clapped and clapped, and Barbara and I were very proud of her.

Then our son Kent, who had learning disabilities and wasn't able to memorize the alphabet until the fourth grade, and his class came out to do their performance. We'll never forget it.

We had worked with Kent on his four lines since Thanksgiving. We had gone that week to visit friends in Denair, and all the way up and back in the car, we had practiced his four lines. He had never once said them right. His sisters and his younger brother could say them backward and forward—we could all say them—but Kent hadn't managed them right once.

The night of his performance, when he went out onto the stage to do his part, we were on the edge of our seats. To everyone else there, I'm sure he just looked like a really nervous kid (which he was), but we were watching him as our dear son. Finally, the spotlight was on him, and he had to say his lines. And he did it! He said, "Strange feelings come upon me, though I know not why. The night is still around me; stars shine in the sky." He did it! He had never done it once, but he managed to do it that night.

And the terrible thing was that Barbara and I were sitting there in the audience, and we couldn't clap! It was the middle of the scene, and no one was clapping. No one hardly even noticed. But we were so happy for him and so pleased that he had been able to say his part.

The thing we realized that night was that we were very pleased with *both* our children. One did a wonderful job that everyone applauded; the other just appeared to be a nervous kid who managed to get out four lines. But we were rejoicing in our hearts.

We pastors have to realize that God our Father sees us the way Barbara and I saw our children. In a sense, God doesn't care about the part He's given us. What He cares about is that we do the best we can at the part He has assigned.

For each of us, right now it's the middle of the play. We're pilgrims on this earth, and reward from our Father in heaven is coming. No one is applauding at this moment. But God sees everything, and our heart attitude is what He cares about.

What If?

How would my life have been different if I had started that church with the $50,000 and the 20 families, and within 6 months there were 400-500 people, and then in another year there had been a thousand? How might my life have been changed if I hadn't experienced the downturn and depression I mentioned earlier in this chapter?

In fact, at that time I sought some counsel from a good friend, and he said, "I'm glad your church didn't grow. If it had, you would have been insufferable. You would have put together a seminar, traveled around the country, and told everyone how to do it." He was saying that if I—given who I was—had been blessed with such growth, I probably wouldn't have developed the requisite humility. My feet wouldn't have stayed on the ground. I wouldn't have depended on the Holy Spirit. The qualities that come through difficult circumstances wouldn't have been built into my life. So it has been sanctifying for me. Now, I also have to say it was a miserable time! But one of the beautiful things about it is that God has used it over the years to encourage hundreds of my brothers and sisters. Thus, it was worth it.

Again, we have to derive our definitions from God's Word, because Jesus said, "Take my yoke upon you and learn from me, . . . for my yoke is easy and my burden is light." What He meant is that the proper burden is one we can carry; but when we try to carry the burden the world places on our shoulders, it's impossible. So we have to carry only the biblical burden.

> Fear not, for I have redeemed you;
>   I have summoned you by name; you are mine.
> When you pass through the waters, I will be with you;
>   and when you pass through the rivers,
>   they will not sweep over you.

When you walk through the fire,
  you will not be burned;
  the flames will not set you ablaze.
For I am the LORD, your God,
  the Holy One of Israel, your Savior. . . .
Do not be afraid, for I am with you. (Isa. 43:1-3, 5)

As we go through the deep waters in ministry, remember that their purpose is not to drown us but to cleanse us.

Pastor *to* Pastor

Pastor, please take a moment to look at the following quotation from Dr. Dobson's book What Wives Wish Their Husbands Knew About Women. *It summarizes well what I believe we should feel about the issue of success.*

> *I have concluded that the accumulation of wealth, even if I could achieve it, is an insufficient reason for living. When I reach the end of my days, a moment or two from now, I must look backward on something more meaningful than stocks and bonds. Nor is fame of any lasting benefit. I will consider my earthly existence to have been wasted unless I can recall a loving family, a consistent investment in the lives of people, and an earnest attempt to serve the God who made me. Nothing else makes much sense.*

My prayer for you, your family, and your future ministry is that you will come to understand that we just can't keep looking over God's shoulder to see what He has next for us. We need to look Him square in the eye and see what He has to say to us today. On the fledgling day of my ministry, I took as my personal Scripture one of the most-quoted in all the Old Testament—Proverbs 3:5-6: "Trust in the Lord with all your heart and lean not unto your own understanding. In all your ways acknowledge Him and He will direct your path." I praise Him for that, and may you find His counsel relevant for this moment in time, my friend.

H. B. L.

I grew up in a tradition where ministers would often greet one another with the questions "How many did you have in Sunday school?" "What kind of offering did you receive?" "How many new members did you take into fellowship?" It was as if they were playing a numbers game. There was a stage, in my middle years of pastoring, during which a good Sunday was more than any other way determined by numbers—not souls won to Christ. I have agonized over that and prayed many times for God to forgive me for my improper motivation. But the truth is, for a large number of pastors, the church has become like any other game that's determined by how many, how much, and for how long.

In deference to many in the church world, we arrived at this point quite innocently. The church-growth movement, pressure from various denominational headquarters, and competition within the Body have created a grow-at-any-cost mentality. All of a sudden, we can become as T. S. Eliot warned, "A people doing the right thing for the wrong reason." I honestly believe that the church of the twenty-first century will be known more by its health than its size. We'll see.

Oh, don't get me wrong. The church—every church—should grow, but for all the right reasons. What if all of us could report at the conclusion of every Sabbath weekend, "The Lord added to the church daily those who were being saved." Or at least, "I provided an opportunity for those who were present to turn their lives over to the Lord." I urge you to read carefully what George Barna has to say about growth, vision, and change as it relates to the local church. The "Pastor to Pastor" edition from which this interview was taken, "Changing Trends in the Ministry," has been one of our most popular to date.

I first learned of George Barna through reading his best-selling book The Frog in the Kettle. *Since then, he has written so many volumes that it's difficult to keep track of them all, but George has caused us to look honestly at ourselves. He has urged us to ask of our own ministry and that of our total church body—why? Why is it working? Why doesn't it work? I really do appreciate the effort George makes to hold the mirror in front of us. I remember telling him one time, "George, if your statistics are just make-believe and you're playing some cruel joke on us, you're going to burn hotter than anyone." He laughed! The church is so much more than numbers, isn't it? But because everyone counts, we must count, and count on everyone.*

H. B. London Jr.

Leaders, Vision, and Success

by George Barna

The only place where the church of Jesus Christ is not growing significantly is North America and the continent of Europe. In every other part of the world, the number of Christians is growing. Why do you think this is so?

From my research and conversations with pastors, I would like to suggest three probable causes of our low growth rate. The first is that we've gone astray when it comes to measuring the success or health of a church. As I've talked to pastors, and as my company has interviewed them in our studies, one thing consistently hits me between the eyes. When you ask a pastor, "How's your church doing?" the usual answer you get is a number. But I can't find anywhere in Scripture where God said, "Thou shalt be successful when thou hast 2,000 or more people in thine church."

Numbers can be an important indication of what's going on in a church, but a number as an answer to the above question is still problematic, because God has called us to be His reflection in the world in order to transform lives. When that transformation is taking place, numbers may be a result. But we shouldn't be shooting for numbers as the ultimate end of the church. In our undying quest for numbers, we sometimes lose sight of the most important things that we're called to do in ministry.

A second cause of low growth in most churches is that the pastor and the congregation don't have a clear sense of God's vision for the ministry. Until that vision has been clarified, articulated, and owned by the congregation as their very heartbeat—as the thing they want to be most obedient to; as something they want to exude tremendous passion for—the church is really going to struggle. If there's no such vision or mission, you become just a caretaker church. You merely put in your time. And we really don't need that kind of church.

The third cause of low growth is that we have many pastors and people in positions of authority within the church who are managers but not leaders. I've seen that for an organization to make headway, to be really meaningful and significant, there has to be a leader who is bringing the people along. Unless that leader is in place, the church isn't going anywhere.

Leaders

Let's look first at the need for leaders.

In my more than 10 years of gathering statistics and visiting churches, the most encouraging thing I see is that a new generation is coming into the ranks of leadership, and these new leaders have an increasing willingness to take risks. That's heartening because the church in this country is not going to reach its potential until we're willing to try new things. Some of those things are going to fail, of course, but that failure will teach us additional lessons. So I'm encouraged by the fact that increasingly church leaders are saying, "Yeah, let's explore some new avenues. Let's try to be creative."

That openness to change doesn't necessarily mean we throw out the old traditions. It may mean there's just a new way of explaining those traditions or exposing them to the people.

If that's the most encouraging thing my research has shown, the most discouraging thing also has to do with leaders. It's this: Most churches in this country don't have leaders at the helm. Until we get people who actually have leadership gifts and skills at the helm of the church, we're playing a dangerous game. Many pastors, by their own admission, don't have those gifts and skills. They have a heart to serve God; they have tremendous abilities. But those abilities aren't necessarily in leadership.

For an analogy, look at what they do in our colleges and universities. When somebody is a great professor, they bump him or her into the administration. Frankly, that's a wonderfully dumb idea! If the person's a great teacher, let him or her teach, and let somebody else push the paper.

But that's frequently what we do in the ministry, too. When we have a great teacher, we expect him to also be an administrator, a manager, a visionary—all those kinds of things. But the individual doesn't necessarily have those gifts. Can he still minister? Absolutely, and with tremendous effect. But he may not have the ability to lead a church the way it needs to be led.

What's the answer? The key thing is to recognize that it's really not the call of the pastor to do all the ministry. It is the pastor's call to empower the laity to do the ministry. So as you look at what you're seeking to do through your church, ask yourself, *Have I designed a ministry structure that allows me to use my gifts, knowledge, energy, and resources to prepare people for realistic, practical, life-changing kinds of ministry?*

In a way, I'm talking about redefining the traditional answer to the question "What is success for a pastor?" It's not numbers; it's not budgets; it's not the size of the staff. It's how many people you can point to and say, "As a result of having been connected to that person in this spiritual family, I have seen his life transformed. I know that when I leave this place, it's almost not going to matter—not because I didn't have any impact, but because I had so much impact by empowering people and encouraging them through God's grace and power that they now *are* the ministry. They're doing it! My primary function was to encourage them, lead them, and continue to challenge them. But I know that when I leave, the ministry here is going to live on."

Perhaps the greatest hindrance to the church's ministry and outreach as we move into the twenty-first century is the lack of knowledge among its members. Consequently, the church needs leaders who will teach their people.

Think of the whole concept of worship. Our studies indicate that most adults in this country have no idea what worship means. Even people who profess to be committed followers of Jesus Christ can't articulate any understanding of the term. And this lack of knowledge is a consistent problem through all the dimensions of ministry in America. Put bluntly, most American Christians are poorly schooled in the basics of their faith.

When we talk with Christians about evangelism, for instance, we find that decreasing numbers are willing to share their faith, and that's because they have a misunderstanding of how the process works. Most of them think that when they share the gospel with somebody, if the person doesn't drop to his or her knees and say the sinner's prayer, their witnessing has been a failure. They don't understand that it's not we who convert somebody but the Holy Spirit.

The basic understandings of the Christian faith are so critical for us leaders to get across to our people. So, rather than worrying about some of the higher theological principles that we occasionally try to get across, we should just get people to understand basics like how prayer works, the importance of worship, what worship really is, why they ought to be in some kind of discipling relationship, what it means to be committed to the church, and why sin still exists today.

Vision

Let's look now at the lack of vision as a cause of low growth.

Perhaps you're a young, idealistic seminary graduate who just can't wait to get out there in the trenches and change the world overnight. Or maybe you're discouraged and lack energy because you've been a pastor for a number of years, and you see the megachurch in your area with its thousands of people, but your church has only 20, 30, 60, or 70 people. In either case, remember that the call of God is on your life. I want to help you see that it's not how many people who come to your church that matters, but what you give to them, the life you live in front of them, and the changes you help to bring about in the families God brings under your teaching and influence.

Whatever your situation, before you do anything else, really understand God's vision for your ministry. Before you run out and do more ministry, understand what your priorities and gifts are, what the call on your life is, so that what you do doesn't just become a job, and so that you don't get burned out because you had unrealistic expectations.

Realize also, however, that if you're going to achieve any kind of success in life, you're going to pay a major price for it. That statement is more true in the ministry than in anything else, because in the ministry, you're not just battling with other people (as you might be in the marketplace). Here you're battling with the powers of darkness, and you have to be prepared to wage spiritual warfare if you're going to be in the ministry for the long haul. You need to prepare yourself for that battle by understanding God's vision for your ministry.

In my case, I began by managing political campaigns. When I kind of burned out in that field, I said, "I need to specialize in something." The two things I enjoyed most were speech-writing and polling, so I decided to concentrate in the polling arena, which I did for a couple of years. After I went to graduate school and picked up some degrees in polling, I got involved in the marketing research industry, working for a large company.

While I was there, a Christian media-management company working with a number of televangelists asked us to do some media testing for them. Nobody in our company was a Christian, so the company had no idea what the Christian company was talking about when it mentioned the Holy Spirit and other Christian things!

Finally, though, my boss (who was in on the negotiations) said, "Wait a minute! We've got that new kid, that Barna guy, who said he's a Christian. Why don't we bring him in? Maybe he can translate for us." So I did. I was a new Christian at the time, and that was my introduction to all the different kinds of ministries being done.

I was so fascinated by it that I eventually took a job with the Christian media-management company I mentioned above and built up a research division for them. Then, after several years, I felt God calling my wife and me to start the Barna Research Group, which was meant to be a state-of-the-art company doing research for ministries so they can make better decisions.

Barna Research has been around for more than 10 years now. But it wasn't until a few years ago that people really found us. And that "being found" has a lot to do with God helping me understand what my vision for ministry needed to be.

We had been working primarily with parachurch ministries and some churches up to that point, and I became really frustrated with them in comparison to the secular organizations with which we were also working, like Visa and First Interstate. One day, I called a staff meeting and said, "You know, guys, this is just tearing me apart. I really want to work for the church, but they frustrate me to no end. They want everything cheap; they don't pay their bills; and then they don't pay attention to the information we give them. That's it! We're not working with them anymore."

Maybe you've felt that way with your elders or your congregation recently! Anyway, my wife and I went on a vacation about a month afterward. I was lying on the beach—praying and soaking in the sun—when for the first time in my life I felt God speak clearly to me. The essence of His message was, "Do you really think I've given you the resources, the contacts, and the opportunities you've had to work with the church so you can turn your back on them because they're tough? Are you kidding Me?" So I came back home, called another staff meeting, and said, "All right, I was wrong."

That shaping of my vision totally reworked how we've done our research. Instead of focusing on large parachurch ministries, at that point we said, "We've got to work with the local church and try to help pastors learn how they can understand their culture and how they can minister in it without compromising the truth." That's how we started to get a higher profile. It began with a reshaping of my vision.

The key thing for pastors, too, really isn't having a 15-year plan but having God's vision for your ministry, because that vision is going to be your constant as you face a changing culture. That vision will be the thread that runs through your entire ministry—the thing that maintains your sense of passion and urgency about your call to the ministry. It will keep you encouraged even in some of the really difficult challenges you'll face. Then your vision, not numbers, will help you judge if you're being a success.

In some ways, the family is a perfect model. Think about it: How do we determine who's a great parent? We don't look at the person who had the most children! We look for the person whose children went out and did good and decent things in life. We look for the parents of children who grew into mature and responsible adults, who added something to society.

Who's the effective pastor? It's not necessarily the one who has the most names on the church rolls. It's probably the one who got the most people excited about Jesus Christ—excited enough that they would sacrifice some of their comforts and opportunities to go out and serve Christ with all they have.

And that goes right back to the question "What is ministry all about?" It's not about numbers; it's about people; it's about relationships. Ministry really has its greatest impact in somebody's life when there's a one-to-one relationship that is growing and thriving.

Again, I keep coming back to the whole concept of modeling. It's hard to model authentic Christianity for people you don't really know! You see somebody from afar, and you may pick up a few pointers. But what astounds people—what leaves a lasting impression—is when they know somebody and they see, in life's tough situations, how that person's faith has made a difference in how he responds.

So we gather research information, and you use it to understand the people to whom you're called to minister. You see, one of the important elements of effective communication is to understand where the person you're trying to evangelize or disciple is coming from. In fact, the only time you can communicate anything well is when you understand that person's perceptual filter and the assumptions he's bringing into the communication process. Our research helps pastors and church leaders reassess what that perceptual filter is and what the assumptions are of the people you want to reach.

Here's an example. A lot of people are talking about a new spiritual sensitivity in America. They refer to the great number of baby boomers who are coming back to the church after having left it in their twenties. But they're not coming back to the traditional church. Some of them are going to the independent churches and the megachurches. But we're sensing, through our admittedly blunt research instruments (because spirituality is a hard thing to get a grip on), that there is, indeed, a huge—maybe even unprecedented—spiritual hunger in America today. The difficulty in this is that the boomers and the busters (the generation that follows the boomers) are not looking to Christianity to answer their spiritual hunger.

We're in an environment now where, because of the information proliferation, people are exposed to all kinds of different faiths. And increasingly, they're picking and choosing elements from each of the different faiths they're exposed to and putting them together into a personalized blend of religion. Technically, this is called syncretism. Christianity is just one of seven or eight faiths that people look at, and then they choose parts of Christianity that they like.

One consequence of this trend is that the average pastor stands in his pulpit addressing specific beliefs that are traditional and absolute for him, but they're not traditional or absolute for the people in his audience. The average boomer or buster has grown up saying, "I don't appreciate tradition. It's not something I understand." So if your church wants to incorporate traditions and absolute beliefs into the life of its ministry, it has to make those traditions and beliefs relevant and alive for the boomers and busters. We can't assume that when a person comes into the church, he's going to understand or embrace your beliefs simply because the church says they're good or meaningful.

Here's another example. Sixty-seven percent of the adults in this country don't believe there is such a thing as absolute truth. Even a majority of the people who claim Christ as their Savior don't believe it!

Now, when you're in a society where that's the case, you have to think about the implications for the whole concept of sin. If there's no such thing as absolute truth, there can be no such thing as sin, because what's a sin for me is not necessarily a sin for you or anybody else. Thus, everything becomes relative. When I propose to someone that Jesus Christ is the answer to life's most serious problems, it's easy for the person to reject it, because according to his or her philosophy of life, there can be no such thing as *the* answer.

Consequently, another thing we have to do in ministry in America today is to reassess how we can communicate truth to a population that doesn't even believe truth exists! Evangelism in this situation isn't necessarily any more difficult than it used to be; but it is different from what it used to be. And we need effective communication, part of which is knowing the other person's perceptual filter and assumptions.

Instead of going out and saying, "You must believe in God. You must believe in Jesus Christ because the Bible says so, and the Bible is absolute truth," we need to take a couple of steps back and say, "Okay, if this person doesn't believe in such a thing as a holy, omnipotent God, and if he doesn't believe the Bible is absolute truth, those are his assumptions. Now, where do I start to help him understand that this is absolute truth?"

Ultimately, we're going to come to a more Socratic approach in which we allow people to work through (in a nonthreatening manner) questions that go to the heart of their philosophy of life. "Do you really believe that? Then how does that work out in the rest of your life?"

All this ties in with the fact that most Americans don't have a thought-out philosophy of life. Only when they start to question what they say they think do they realize, "This philosophy that I guess I've been operating with—that there is no truth; that there is no God or there are many gods—that stuff just doesn't work."

But when you give it to them as, "Here, I've got the answer," they usually reject you and your message. We have to ask them those piercing questions.

Sometimes I'm criticized when people say that in my statistical harvesting, I circumvent the Holy Spirit, the miraculous, and the supernatural—and that everything may not follow a trend. Let me say, though, that there's nothing we can do to serve God and glorify Him outside His power. He has to be the center of what we're doing. And I would never counsel anybody to use any technique or strategy that minimizes God's hand or the working of the Holy Spirit. He is sovereign. I am not, nor are our techniques and information. They're tools to be used for God's glory.

Change

Our studies show that understanding for, appreciation of, and respect for the average minister have reached all-time lows. People's trust in the clergy to understand and deal with their problems and to lead them has been consistently declining over the past 15 years or so. It's not because of the televangelist scandals. (Our research shows that Americans have abundantly short memories.) It's because the expectations for ministers are very different from what they were 20 or 25 years ago. At that time, we looked to pastors to dispense theological knowledge and manage the services and programs of the church.

Today, we're called to minister within a much more sophisticated, fast-paced, information-driven, market-driven atmosphere. And that different atmosphere requires a different mind-set (or a different perspective) and, in some ways, a different set of skills and techniques. The pastor needs to have the same heart, but a different application.

The statistics showing the paradigm shifts, the mood shifts, and so forth for the baby boomers, the baby busters, and now Generation X can cause some pastors to say, "How can I relearn all this? How can I ever be the kind of pastor I evidently have to be according to what the research says people want?"

Essentially, we have to understand that we're always students. No matter how many degrees we have, we always have to be learning, because our environment for ministry is constantly changing. People have different needs and expectations. We have different resources and challenges. And figuring out how to put them all together and balance them requires a constant state of learning and growth.

At the point when a plant stops growing, that's essentially when it dies. Until then, it has to change constantly (every second it has any life in it). That's the way we need to see ourselves and our ministries, too: They have to be constantly changing. We can't compromise the truth, but we have to be constantly rethinking, asking ourselves, *How do I relate to people better? How do I position and structure my ministry better? How can I be more effective for Christ?*

As we work with different ministries and secular organizations, we're telling them, "It's kind of crazy to have something like a 20-year plan, because at this point in our history, the society is basically redesigning itself (reinventing itself, if you will) on a 3-to-5-year cycle. If you try to project more than 3 to 5 years ahead, you're really wasting your time."

What you have to do is try to figure out what's going to happen in the next 12 months that you can strategically prepare yourself for—and maybe think even a couple of years beyond that. But to put a lot of energy and resources into thinking way down the line is probably a waste. And remember, what you want is God's vision for your ministry.

Are You in a Small Church?

I want to encourage the pastors of small churches, because that's where most Americans go to church. We did a study with unchurched people a few years ago, and one thing we found was that the majority of unchurched people would rather go to a church of 200 or fewer people. That study raises the question, "Well, then, why do most of those people actually wind up at larger churches?" There are a couple of reasons.

One is that most of the large churches grow big because the people in them are inviting their friends to come to church with them. You can't have a church that's meeting people's needs unless the people who make up the church are serious about doing ministry. We can't have a church that's really effective if we expect the pastor to do all the ministry. Frequently, what you find in small churches is that the people are kind of a cheering section on Sundays. They come out to see the pastor do his performance, they cheer, they put their money in the plate, and they walk out.

Second, other studies we've done show that most small churches don't grow because the people in them don't want them to grow. They're happy with the small group of people who are there. They don't want outsiders coming in and changing the dynamics, the needs, and the facilities. They want things to stay the way they are because they, like most of us, tend to resist change.

There's a place, then, for the small church. But it requires a different perspective on leadership, a whole distinct kind of dynamic in terms of how we get people to relate to one another, and a different approach to how we explain and train people for ministry.

Gearing Up for the Future

The majority of unchurched adults in America are singles. What's the church going to do with them?

First, we have to recognize there are three distinct populations of singles: those who have never been married, those who have been married and divorced, and those who have been widowed. Altogether, they compose about 45 percent of the population today—and they will be the majority in the future.

But each of the three subgroups has a different profile and set of needs. The common thread that runs through all of them is the need for relationships. But the church has to be careful about how it allows relationships to develop in the lives of singles. Handling independence is another element. In the case of single parents (which is one of the faster-growing populations and the one that consistently tells us, "When I needed the church, it wasn't there!"), there's a whole dimension of acceptance without judgment that we have to learn about.

Women in the church are another group to think about for the future. We would be unwise to speak for each woman individually, but among women as a population, in the next 10 years, we'll see an increasing interest in and demand for responsibility and authority. We have to be prepared to deal with those issues. We're going to find increasing numbers of women in the work force, too, even women with young children. We have to understand what it means for the Christian community to serve a woman who has a young child, who is married, who is in the work force, and who has all kinds of other things going on as well.

We have to figure out how we can make the Bible relevant to an individual who is going through such dramatic transformations in her lifestyle. That's one of the difficulties so many woman are having, and that's why small-group Bible studies are so popular among women. They're one of the ways they can come together and discuss some of the tough issues of faith.

We must also think about the urban church and how to help it. Those of us in suburban or rural churches have a responsibility to the urban church. We're going to find that as the cities become increasingly minority-based, they're not going to have a huge pool of resources, yet they are going to have a huge degree of need.

We must not make the mistake, however, of looking at the urban population as a single group. It still has a tremendous number of Caucasians, but it will increasingly be a blend of blacks, Hispanics, and Asians. Each of those populations has a different set of values, lifestyles, and felt needs. Each church that's trying to minister to one of those populations will have to understand the uniqueness of that community and how it can make the gospel relevant in that context without compromise.

$50,000,000,000

In 1992, more than $50 billion was spent on ministry within the United States. But the statistics show that only 2 out of 10 people who join churches are new converts. Basically, our growth comes from people moving from one church to another, not by conversion. That's really not the way the church is meant to grow.

When I talk with pastors, what I frequently hear is, "Well, we could do great things if we only had the money." Money isn't really the issue, however. The money is there. You can't tell me we can't do astounding things with $50 billion! The real question is, how are we using that money? Have we identified our priorities? Have we figured out how to use our resources strategically?

Also, are we really operating as a movement of God, or are we functioning as about 300,000 individual fiefdoms? That's the number of Protestant churches in this country. I wonder if we couldn't be more effective if we learned how to work cooperatively. In spite of some of our theological differences, ultimately we exist for the same basic purposes. Wouldn't it be something if every church in a city realized that this was its city and its responsibility, so that together they all decided to share their gifts, finances, and talents in order to touch that city for Christ?

When you pray for revival, make that a part of your prayer.

Pastor *to* Pastor

The Bible tells us of David in 1 Samuel 18:14, "In everything he did he had great success, because the LORD was with him." I sincerely hope George Barna's comments will make the term success *a little less threatening for you.*

I also hope you feel encouraged by the suggestion that in a world where almost everything changes, God's mission for His church does not. We praise God that His love and grace are never-changing as well.

Let me share an encouraging note with you that one pastor's wife gave him after he had left his assignment because of doctrinal disagreements with his denomination. This man left the pastorate, not knowing what work they would do next or even how they would put food on the table. They moved their family in with relatives and then trusted the Lord and His leading. The following is her note to him on his birthday, less than two months after their move.

> *A wonderful happy birthday to you! I hope you have a special day commensurate with how special you are!*
>
> *Remember that true "success" in life comes from putting God first and doing His will. His approval is more important than that of any man. Thanks for your godly example and leadership.*
>
> *I emptied my wallet for you! You may even spend this on a book!*
>
> *I love you.*

And remember, pastor, God keeps on loving you! Hang in there! It's not a numbers game. It's a relational thing. The better the relationship we have with our Lord, the greater the success in His eyes!

H. B. L.

10

I was 23 years old and fresh out of graduate school when I assumed "leadership" of my first pastorate in South Whittier, California. Was I ever in for a surprise! The congregation was not impressed with a seminary education or the fact I had interned in some good-sized churches. And it really didn't matter to them that I represented the fourth generation in my family to serve in full-time Christian service.

Naturally, all this concerned me a bit, because I had the impression that as their pastor, I would also be their respected and valued leader. That was not to be. The real leader was a senior adult with little education who worked nights as a custodian at a local elementary school. He lived in a small house, drove an old car, and had minimal influence anywhere else, but he was the "key man" in our church of around 50 people. His name was Brother Tresner, and like the television commercial by E. F. Hutton, when he spoke, everyone listened. Even me.

Probably you've had the same rude awakening in some of your assignments. John Maxwell certainly has. You'll enjoy his comments on what constitutes leadership. I've learned that the longer a pastor stays in one place, the more likely he is to be the influencer, but at the start, you must earn it the old-fashioned way. Some of our colleagues never stay anywhere long enough to be the major influence in their churches, and as a result, a lot of them never feel fulfilled in their place of service.

In 1968, I moved to Salem, Oregon, and for the next 17 years I served a great church in that community. Only after about 6 or 7 years there did I realize what it meant to be a trusted influencer/leader of a congregation. For most of you, too, it will take that long. John Maxwell will agree.

I first met John when we were both young pastors. He came to Salem to pick my brain. We sat for a considerable amount of time in Denny's restaurant and talked about ministry style and philosophy. We were both of a tradition that had not known many "mega" churches. Our time together was shortly before he would assume the role as pastor of Skyline Wesleyan Church in San Diego. The rest is history. I can say with a great deal of confidence that there are few people in the church world today who "influence" the way pastors pastor as does John Maxwell.

H. B. London Jr.

Leadership in the Church

by John Maxwell

Pastors are preachers—and where would we be if we knew we couldn't preach well? Pastors are also shepherds, and we must feed and protect the flock. We administer the sacraments, too, and along with the other leaders of the church, we're to teach and correct in the congregation. There are, of course, countless other duties and tasks that fall upon us as pastors. One of them is leadership.

Leadership Is Influence

Leadership is influence. It's that simple. The person with the most influence in any given group at any given time is the leader of that group at that time. The problem is that we pastors haven't been taught that definition. Instead, we're taught that leadership is position or title. And with that definition enters in the frustration, because we then—as "the pastor"—go into a church and think we're "the leader."

For example, in my denomination, the book of order said I (as pastor) was the chairman of the board of the church. If I didn't know better, then, I would think I was literally the leader. But if I walked into a board meeting, as chairman, I only got to open up the meeting. Then the real leader would take over!

My first church was just a handful of people in a rural setting. I was the pastor of that church for three years and three months, but I was never the leader of the church. I never became the prominent influencer within that church body.

I was in my second church, which was more of a medium-sized church, for three or four years before I became the prominent influencer there.

In any congregation, there will be laypeople who have been at that church for years—having seen pastors come and pastors go—and they will not be about to give the pastor the leadership of the church. In some cases, they see their leadership in that church as their mark in society—sometimes their *only* mark—and they won't even think about relinquishing it.

Establishing Leadership

What, then, should we do to establish leadership in a congregation?

First, we have to accept the fact that leadership is influence.

Second, we need to ask ourselves, *Who are the influencers?* In a church of 100 or less, there will usually be no more than 5 influencers. But we have to identify who they are.

Third, we have to ask ourselves, *Whom do these influencers influence? Do they sway the whole church or a part of the church?* At this stage we begin to segment the church, based on whom the influencers oversee.

In a small church, it's much easier for one person to influence the whole congregation. When you get into churches in the hundreds and thousands, it's impossible for one layperson to direct the whole church. Instead, one influencer will affect the church through the music department, another through the Christian education department, and so on.

Fourth, we need to ask, *What is the key to each influencer's life?* If we find those keys, we can go to each influencer and become a friend of that person. Then we can influence the influencers.

Think of the seeker-sensitive approach, the use of small groups, and all the other themes that are going around the church world today. So often we pastors go to conferences on these current themes, but when we come back to our churches, because we aren't the leader, we never "sell" the new paradigm. And sometimes we destroy our right to extend our stay in that congregation in the process. We come back with a hot idea, but we don't teach it to our people in a good way—we just throw it out there in front of them. We don't go through our influencers. All of a sudden, the influencers balk, and we've lost our ministry. I've seen it happen way too many times.

Insecurity: A Pastor's Greatest Deficit

The greatest deficit the average pastor faces is insecurity. If we're insecure and unwilling to give someone else credit or to work through other people (our influencers), we're going to be in trouble.

For example, I've mentioned that my first church was small. (In fact, the first day we had Sunday school, when it was time to begin, only three people were present—and my wife and I were two of them!) As I worked in that church, I learned quickly that the major influencer was a man named Claude. He was a farmer, and he didn't analyze things to figure out he was the leader, but he was nonetheless. He was the prominent influencer in that whole rural community.

I recognized Claude's leadership, and I began to work on the farm with him during the week before every board meeting. As we worked, we'd share ideas. Then I would let him take all the ideas we talked about to the board. The board believed every idea that came into the meetings was Claude's. I never told them different, never brought up an idea myself. That dear brother literally took care of everything for me.

Now, here's an example of insecurity. When I got ready to leave that

Stuart Briscoe

The qualifications of a pastor:

1. The mind of a scholar.
2. The heart of a child.
3. The hide of a rhinoceros.

church, I sat down with the man who was going to follow me as pastor. I had gone to college with him and knew him well. I told him how I had tried to influence the influencer, with considerable success. And I'll never forget how the new pastor sat up, pointed at me, and said, "That may be the way you ran the church, but if and when I come there, *I'm* going to be the leader of the church."

My heart sank, because I knew he was in trouble.

The insecure pastor trumpets his title. The secure pastor is a servant leader who's willing to work through other people and let them have the credit for his ideas.

Integrity: The Most Important Ingredient of Leadership

If leadership is influence, its most important ingredient is integrity.

Today the word *integrity* has been brought into question simply because no one knows how to define it exactly. At its root, though, integrity is not what we do as much as who we are.

Too many times, when we think of leadership, we think of charisma—of a dynamic personality. But while charisma may get you in through the door of the church, it won't keep you there. *Credibility* is the *only* thing that will keep you there. Credibility establishes trust—when what I say and what I do match up. So we pastors have to sit back and ask ourselves, *Am I role-playing? Am I really the person I'm presenting on Sunday morning? Am I personally enjoying the life I'm asking my people to live, or is this sermon just a message and this service just an event?*

Here's the acid test based on extensive experience: If you and I really have credibility, then the longer we stay in a church, the better things will get in the areas of trust and personal relationships. But if we lack credibility, the longer we stay, the worse those areas will become. The church will begin to tear and pull apart at the seams.

Accountability: A Necessary Part of Integrity

Any great leader who has integrity has someone to hold him in account, be that "someone" a group of people, one man, or a covenant-relationship partner. But there must be someone who's not afraid to ask the tough questions.

I've seen too many wonderful pastors whom I looked up to as my heroes bite the dust, spiritually speaking. Consequently, I'm scared for all pastors.

I'll never forget something Howard Hendricks said. He had done a survey of pastors who had fallen, and he had learned three things. First, the pastors who fell were not in the Word, and they weren't practicing their daily walk with God as they needed to be doing. Second, they never thought they would experience spiritual failure. And third, they weren't accountable to anyone.

Those findings stood me on my ears! I had been one of those guys who thought it would never happen to him! So when I went to Skyline Wesleyan Church in 1981, I sat down with a dear older brother and asked if we could meet monthly. I gave him some questions to ask me about my personal life, my walk with God, and my choices. He wasn't on the church board, and he had no power position in the church, so I couldn't play games with him. He came to my study every month, prayed with me for an hour, and asked me the questions. And the last of them was, "John, have you lied about any of the previous questions?"

Creating Positive Change: The Ultimate Test of Leadership

The ultimate test of leadership is creating positive change. And around the country, in churches of every denomination, the church is going through challenging times in large part because of its inability to accept change.

But it's not just the church. We all resist change! I certainly do. Before I started holding leadership conferences, I assumed that the "leader" was for change and the "followers" were against it. But then I began dealing with pastors, and I found that a lot of us aren't really in favor of change. We're insecure concerning the whole process of change, so we resist it.

Consequently, I began to work hard with leaders to help us understand that the only way we'll ever grow is through change. We—you!—cannot grow without change. Note that I'm not saying "Change means growth," because you can change something and lose it. But growth means change. In fact, the difference between change meaning growth and change meaning grief is the ability of the leader (the pastor) to bring his people through a positive process.

There are three times when people will change. (This is true inside the church as well as outside.) These times are like the tide: they come in, and they go out. You have to seize the moment.

First, people change when they *hurt* enough that they have to change. We've all seen people who are desperate. They run into our study after their spouse has left them and say, "I'll do anything to get my marriage back together." Well, what happened? Did the marriage go bad all of a sudden? No. But the marriage finally got so bad that they hurt enough to be willing to do something to fix it.

Second, people change when they learn enough that they're *able* to change. Here is where I think pastors have their greatest failures. In creating positive change in our churches, we have to expose our people to the benefits of change. I tell pastors at conferences that if they brought a key layman or two—especially influencers—with them to the conference, they're going to be far ahead of the pastors who came alone. Too few times do we include our key influencers on the ground floor of change so they understand the reasons for it from the start.

When Moses' father-in-law, Jethro, told him he needed to change his style of leadership, the first thing Moses did was to bring the whole congregation together and explain the situation.

In Acts 6, when the church leaders realized they could no longer personally serve the widows, they appointed seven men to be deacons. Note, though, the *first* thing they did: They brought the congregation together.

If we fail to expose our people to the process that led up to change and new ideas—even if they're great ideas—the natural tendency of people is to resist the change. So we need to teach people. When they learn enough, they'll want change.

The third time when people are open to change is when they *receive* enough so that they're able to do it. That "receiving enough" could be the power of God's Spirit in our church—a time of renewal and momentum-building. Or it could be a new program or a new ministry tool. But it must be something that "puts us over the top."

We pastors need to understand those moments—and seize them.

Change as a Challenge: Worship and Music

Music and worship have become a great source of frustration to a lot of churches and pastors.

Let's suppose that a young pastor wants to create a change in his church's style of worship and music. He wants to move away from the traditional two hymns, a prayer, a responsive reading, a solo, and a benediction. He's going to try to spice up the service. How should he go about making such changes?

With music, there's always a lot of emotion involved. One thing I tell pastors is that whenever they discover emotional and traditional fences, before tearing them down, they should find out why they are there.

For example, I pastored a basically traditional church, and we had to go through a lot of changes. Here are a couple of things we did that might help other pastors.

We did not do away with hymns. We still had them. But we used the overhead projector instead of hymnals, or we printed the hymns in the bulletin so people would be free to clap with the music if it was upbeat.

We used a worship team to develop the change from people sitting and just hearing a choir perform to a participative kind of worship. And we sent our worship team to a Maranatha seminar. The seminar was powerful, and when the team members came home, they were changed.

Then we started taking between 100 and 200 of our church's key influencers to Maranatha seminars. Again, we were exposing our laypeople to others who did a fine job of teaching about worship, and the laypeople came back with a totally different understanding of why we moved our worship in the new direction.

One of the biggest problems encountered in changing music is that most churches are multigenerational. And every generation has its definite preference in style of worship.

As a pastor in the worship service, I made myself visible to the congregation and worshiped with them. I needed to be *involved* in worship, not just leading it. I didn't want to come walking out and then fumble through my Bible, trying to decide what I was going to say.

I also needed to *model* worship for my people. We even kept spotlights focused on our pastoral staff during the worship service, not as if they were performers, but to model worship for the congregation.

Finally, as Rick Warren has said, "Tell me what kind of music your church likes or has grown up with, and I'll tell you what kind of church you have." He also said, "What is sung is almost more important than what is said." When worship is right, it does for the church in the 1990s what preaching did for the church in the 1980s.

Leading our people in change has great significance. In this case, exposing them to the kinds of music we wanted (as in the Maranatha seminars) and being the model for them really helped them make the necessary changes.

The Attitude of a Leader

Life is 10 percent what happens to us and 90 percent how we react to it. I say that even in view of the testing of attitude many of you are going through as you read these words. You might be giving up rather than saying, "I can change things if I allow God to work through me." I'm seeing that everywhere, and it's probably my biggest burden in working with pastors.

Pastors haven't really had any training in the area of burnout or frustration. I think of a survey from Fuller on pastors' self-image that appeared in *Focus on the Family* magazine. It broke my heart when I realized how low the self-image of pastors is. And when we begin to feel low about ourselves, we start to see everything that happens to us as either an attack on us or an indication that we're failing or we're not deserving. We begin a negative failure cycle.

I work with pastors on attitude more than anything else. And I find a lot of pastors who wish they were somewhere else. This really burdens me. But maybe I was part of the problem. You see, pastors see pastors of large churches who travel around and speak at conferences, and they hear them get up and tell great stories. And then they say, "Wow! There's a success—and I'm not a success. I've got a small church." So I'm saying to pastors, "Don't be a Maxwell! Don't be a Rick Warren! Don't be another Bill Hybels! Be yourself! Be who you are, and don't let anyone squeeze you into a mold. Do you really think that success is having a church of a certain size?"

A pastor once said to me at a conference, "John, you must really be happy. You're in San Diego, and you've got a big church."

I replied, "Let me tell you something. I was as happy in my first church with three people the first Sunday as I am with 3,000 people right now." Happiness doesn't lie in the size of your church.

So maybe pastors of large churches have done an injustice to other pastors. Maybe in trying to help them grow churches, we've set a standard that somehow says, "I can get happy when I have 500" or "I can get happy when I move to the next church." What we have is a bunch of pastors with what I call "destination disease." *They think happiness lies somewhere else.* It breaks my heart.

I say to pastors, "If you can't be happy where you are—if you can't have a good attitude with the people you have now—you're not going to be happy where you're going to go." We have to realize that our attitude—our happiness or lack of it—is a choice. And we must take responsibility for our attitude and determine that (with the strength God gives us) we're going to develop the right attitude.

But how do we get out of a funk? What's the pastor to do who finds himself struggling with his attitude toward the church and the ministry—who finds himself thinking, *I'm getting out of here. I don't deserve this kind of treatment*?

First, he has to realize that every pastor has said those words to himself. Every one of us feels that way sometimes. And those feelings aren't bad; they're natural. But in response, we need to do something unnatural. Here's what I mean: There are two types of people, those who do something only because they feel good about it and those who do something because they know that if they do what's *right*, they'll feel good *later*. One is committed and acts on *character*, while the other is a person of *convenience*. So we must go back to what's *unnatural* and respond not out of emotion or mood, but based on character.

Many times when I've gone out and shared my faith, in the middle of witnessing, I've felt so good that it's been wonderful. But only 30 minutes before that time, I didn't want to share my faith, didn't want to knock on a door, didn't want to make a call.

My *convenience* response was to beg out of that sort of thing! But my *character* response was to do the right thing.

That's true with our preaching as well, by the way. Many times, I didn't feel like preaching. But I would go ahead and preach, and then afterward I would say, "Thank You, God. You used it, and it was good."

What Is Success?

We have an incredible (literally) idea of success. We think success is a number—the attendance number of a church. But it's not that at all.

A few years ago, I told my congregation what I think success is. *Success is having the people who are the closest to me love and respect me the most.*

It's like this: On a given Sunday morning, some 3,000 people came to Skyline Wesleyan Church. And they would thank me for the message, which was wonderful. But when I got into my car and my wife, Margaret, got in, slid over, patted me on the knee, gave me a kiss on the cheek, and said, "Honey—good message. You live this, John. What you said this morning I see every day in our home"—that was success. Or when I got home after four services on a Sunday morning, and I was tired, and one of my children came up and said, "Dad, it was the best message you ever preached," that was success.

Success isn't doing a conference. Success isn't writing a book. Success is going home, being with the people who know you best, and knowing that you love them and they love you. When you think about it, when it comes time for you to die, what do you have? You have your faith, and you have your family.

If you're struggling in this area, please remember that your family is more important than your ministry. Some "successful" men have given more attention to their ministry than to their families. And so the success they have is empty at best.

Too often, we look for strokes from the church to feed our ego instead of seeking the loving relationship we can have with our own family. I used to tell my congregation at least every six months, "I want you to know that I love you. But you are a distant second compared to my family. It's not a race as to who's going to get my attention or my affection. My family is so important." And do you know what? Saying that gave great security to the church.

In fact, if you *need* your congregation—their constant approval—it's hard to lead them.

Keep Focused!

Keep focused! We have to watch out for the old habit of getting our eyes off the Lord and onto people who we think have made it. We begin to envy them and emulate them when we don't have the inside goods or the personality to be who they are. So keep focused! Keep your eyes on the Lord. Keep your hand in your wife's hand; love her; and every day, affirm her and your children. Remember that the building up of your family and the rearing of your children is absolutely the most important thing.

Keep focused! Don't turn around; don't look over your shoulder. Preach Jesus Christ. You're going to win some; you're going to lose some. When you win, if you're not focused, you'll get big-headed and fall. When you lose, if you're not focused, you'll get disillusioned and quit.

The church and the world need leaders who will use their influence at the right time, for the right reasons—leaders who will take a little greater share of the blame and a little smaller share of the credit; who lead themselves successfully before attempting to lead others; who continue to search for the best answer, not just for the familiar or convenient one; who work for the Lord and for the benefit of others and not for personal gain; who handle themselves with their heads and others with their hearts; who know the way, go the way, and show the way; who live with people to know their problems and live with God in order to solve them; who will be as honest in small things as in great things; who discipline themselves so they won't be disciplined by others; who encounter setbacks and turn them into comebacks; and who follow a moral compass that points in the right direction, regardless of the trends.

In this present age, my friend, this final point bears repeating: The church and the world need leaders who will follow a moral compass regardless of trends—or of convenience.

Be a real leader. You are a person of great influence.

Pastor *to* Pastor

Leadership, influence, insecurity, integrity, accountability, the creation of positive change, attitude, success, and focus. Those are the things John Maxwell speaks of in the chapter above. And as important as they all are, they're only a part of what's involved in your busy life as a pastor!

As I looked back over my thirty-some years as a shepherd, I came up with a few comments to help you put it in perspective. Let me share them with you, "pastor to pastor!"

First, I wish I had studied more.

Second, I wish I had been more faithful in my quiet time with the Lord.

Third, I wish I had been a better listener.

Fourth, I wish I had given more attention to the present and a lot less time to bemoaning the past and fretting over tomorrow. (I missed a lot of "happy todays.")

Fifth, I wish I had spent much more time with my family. When you pause to think about it, they matter more than anyone except God.

And finally, I wish I had been able to take myself less seriously. I needed to realize I wasn't indispensable! (I did—but I didn't.)

So, pastor, seek the finer things in your ministry. Keep a genuine smile tucked away somewhere, ready to use in troubling times. God will take care of you! He has made you a leader—a servant leader. Become that leader to the flock God has given to your care!

H. B. L.

11

This chapter may just be the most controversial in the whole book. Its author, by nature, is somewhat controversial, but even more than that, he dares call into question some of the very things for which pastors and Christian leaders are all grasping. Os Guinness calls it "modernity"—a possible substitute for the Holy Spirit. It's not as much the various changes that are taking place within the church, but what those changes are doing to the church. "For better or for worse?" may be the question we should ask of one another as we bow ourselves at the idol of the newest "sacred food." Time alone and the proven quality of your ministry will determine that answer.

I've had many opportunities since 1991 to travel the nation and parts of the world for the purpose of encouraging and hopefully enlightening those in the clergy I meet along the way. What I see and hear from them can be very disconcerting. I've seen more than a few pastors pulling their hair, even doubting themselves, because what they're trying to do for the Kingdom's sake isn't working, or at least their congregation isn't growing as it should.

The result is that in many situations, they go the way of the latest "religious fad." I encounter pastors all over the place who appear to be standing in front of a wall full of levers, pondering which one to choose. Will it be the lever called "seeker sensitive," "contemporary," or maybe "traditional and contemporary"? Should they go independent and leave the security of their denomination? Or maybe they should just leave their established church behind and plant something new. What conference should they attend next? They already have so many tapes and notebooks now that they don't have time to read them or, more importantly, apply them. "Help me!" they're crying out.

Honest, pastor, I'm not being cynical or in any way attempting to malign your motives or your circumstances. I'm simply asking you to be the person God has called you to be. Use your best gifts, love your people, forget what's happening down the street, and find satisfaction in knowing God is pleased with you. I beg you not to be intimidated by modernity. Os Guinness makes a powerful statement in *this chapter when he writes, "We have come to rely on the tools rather than the Lord." I admit we must take a statement like that in context, but as you read further, I beg you, plead with you, to examine closely what it's costing you to do what you're doing. It may be that church growth and ministerial prominence can be achieved without God or, in time, no need for God. Heaven forbid!*

H. B. London Jr.

Being a Pastor in the Modern World

by Os Guinness

Pastors are the key to much of the hope for the church in the future. Yet many pastors are demoralized today; or, if they're not demoralized, they are truly in danger of pursuing the latest insights and technologies of modernity uncritically.

The Positive Possibilities of Modernity

And what is modernity? Although it's a new word to many people, it's not all that complicated. After I gave a speech on the topic at the Lausanne Conference on evangelism in Manila, a dear woman came up to me and said, "I didn't hear all you said, and I didn't understand all I did hear; but why on earth did they ask a *man* to speak on *maternity*?" That humorous incident points to the fact that many people won't know what we mean when we refer to *modernity*.

But just as we know what *mother* and *maternal* mean, and that maternity is the sum total of everything to do with motherhood, in the same way we can know that modernity is the spirit, system, and sum total of everything that make up our "modern" world. That includes satellites, trains, cars, planes, computers, fax machines, e-mail, tape recorders, compact discs, cable television, the Internet, shopping malls—and more. It's a world that has been produced by capitalism and that relies on technology, industry, and modern telecommunications. And the fact is that it's a radically new world, one that has more implications for discipleship and faith than many Christians realize. But it is into this world of modernity that you have been called to be a Christian pastor.

In fact, not only are pastors to minister in this world of modernity, but you are also to minister to a church that has moved into modernity.

The benefits of modernity are countless, and they are evident. I keep going back to the early church's phrase: "God told the children of Israel to plunder the Egyptians, but He judged them for setting up the golden calf." The golden calf was made out of the very gold that God had told the Israelites to get from their Egyptian neighbors, so there was nothing wrong in plundering the Egyptians. In other words, there's nothing wrong with looking at all the modern insights and technologies that are good and saying, "We'll use these." But we must critique them theologically—that is, critique them biblically—and use them in a wise and responsible way. Otherwise, the church is growing by unauthorized means, in the sense that the growth is purely modern growth: It's not spiritual and theological growth.

Modernity can function as a substitute for the Holy Spirit. If a church does not formulate and articulate its mission and vision, within 5 or 10 years, that church will exist simply to support an organization rather than to enlarge on its vision and mission. It has often been said in the past that when the church is doing well under its own steam, the Holy Spirit could withdraw entirely and the church would go on for a long time without anyone noticing. The modern world really makes that possible.

Let me put it this way. The challenge in the Scripture is not to live by bread alone, but by every word that proceeds from the mouth of the Lord. Our entire culture, though, can be said to be built around the principle of living by bread alone—that is, by reason alone, by technique alone, by sex alone, by marketing alone.

You have the possibility of huge, growing churches that have nothing to do with a daily reliance on the Holy Spirit. And they could go on that way for decades. There's literally no need for God when you use the best management insights so brilliantly. But to misuse the tools and techniques of modernity is certainly wrong.

Warnings Against the Misuse of Modernity

Peter Berger has said, "He who sups with the devil of modernity had better have a long spoon." In other words, modernity gives us wonderful gifts; but if we come to rely on those gifts and not on the Lord, they become idols, because they replace our trust and confidence in the Lord alone.

The key thing is this, however: Many people think that modernity is dangerous where it's hostile, and sometimes it is (as it is in, say, secularization, that aspect of modernity which drives religion to the margins of life). But the real danger of modernity is not where it's hostile, but where it's wonderfully beneficial. In other words, its insights and tools are so powerful and so brilliant that we use them, naturally. That's the first stage. Then, in the second stage, we come to rely on them, and eventually, in the final stage, we have no need of God.

For example, 50 years ago, if you wanted to start a new church or a new missionary initiative, you might have prayed, consulted with people, waited on the Lord, looked at a place to go, and so on. Today, you just run demographic statistics through a computer, and you immediately know where to go and what to do! There's nothing wrong with statistics and computers. It's just that the analyses and computers are so wonderful that you can eventually come to rely on them alone and have absolutely no need of God.

And then, to many modern pastors—sad to say—theology is irrelevant.

Everything has to do with leadership, delegation, and all those good things. But people don't take theology seriously, and evangelicalism in particular is suffering from a desperate form of truth decay. One of the ways the problem shows itself is in a discounting of serious theology. People take theology to be academic, dry, and dusty rather than the royal road to knowing the Lord Himself and the truth of what knowing Him entails.

In many places around the world, the church is growing. The fact is—as statistics tell us—the church of Jesus Christ is growing everywhere but in the United States and on the continent of Europe. In the United States, we're pulling out all the stops that a person can imagine, and still the church has been struggling more in the past decade than it has ever struggled before.

Put it like this: The church is flourishing in the premodern world, but in the world of advanced modernity (where the church is highly modernized), the church is up against it.

This fits with the fact that there are three great storm fronts of modernity: Japan, Western Europe, and the United States. If you put it like that, you see the significance of the United States. Japan, you see, has never been won to Christ, and it's a tough place to evangelize today. Western Europe has been won twice and lost twice. To re-win it today would be an extremely challenging task. And as for the United States, we have tremendous problems here, but the church is still reasonably well off spiritually, financially, numerically, and so on.

So, we can now understand that people should not resort to saying, "Oh, wonderful things are happening in the developing world!" They are, thank God. But they can't naturally and easily be transplanted here, because the developing world is premodern—its countries and peoples have not been through modernism yet.

Our challenge is to stand and be faithful right here and now.

Why Modernity Can Tempt Pastors

Many pastors today are wringing their hands and making themselves sick with worry because their churches have not grown by 10 more people than attendance was last year and because the giving is down. They're watching television and seeing megachurches jam-packed with people—even on the front seats! And these pastors are saying, "If I don't make my church grow, I'm not going to be successful. People won't see me as successful." And certainly one of the idols we must beware of is the idol of a church-growth mentality.

Look at history, though. Traditionally, in the United States, the pastor had a high standing. A town's minister was the "parson" because he was the "person" in the town who was well-educated and a true leader. This line of respect goes all the way back to the Puritans. But in the last hundred years, lawyers and doctors, with their new professional standing, have eclipsed pastors. So the background for the ministry today is one of deep insecurity and social anxiety.

On the one hand, then, the expectations placed on the pastorate are almost impossible to meet. On the other hand, though, the challenges—the tasks a pastor is called to do—are equally impossible. Consequently, you have in today's pastorate one of the highest callings imaginable combined with low possibilities of ever fulfilling the job. This is the background that many pastors struggle against today.

As the church at large faces a crisis, people are almost longing for anything that works. Any new seminar, any new system of doing things that's going around, will be latched onto as a new way of growing churches or whatever. I think that background—that unacknowledged hunger—needs to be dealt with first.

Now, of course, the megachurches and the church-growth people have an enormous number of useful insights. Our critiques are of their excesses, not of the good parts in them. But the excesses are very dangerous excesses.

One of those problems is when their insights are bad in the sense that they're half-truths taken to an unwise extreme. For example, one widely read book on marketing the church speaks of the Bible as a marketing text and says that the audience, not the message, is sovereign. It then develops the whole seeker-friendly, audience-driven type of approach.

Now, is that right or wrong? It's absolutely wrong, biblically speaking. The audience is never sovereign. That's a modern marketing idea that's extremely dangerous. It's a half-truth. The apostle Paul does say, "We become all things to all people to win them to Christ." So step one is identification or contextualization. Yes, we do become one with people: boomers to the boomers, hippies to the hippies, just as we become Chinese to the Chinese and so on. But the audience is not sovereign; the Lord God and the Word of God are sovereign. And if we make the audience sovereign, we sell out the gospel.

That's one example where a half-truth is taken to a dangerous extreme. But there are others, too. Another is what might be described as "the lust for relevance" that many of the megachurches also have. Robert Godfrey has pointed out that the most relevant sermons are those that teach us who God is or that call us to crucify our selfish sin nature and live unselfishly.

By being all things to all people (in the wrong sense of that phrase), though, we dilute our message and run the risk of being nothing to everybody.

When evangelicals do this, they're recycling the old problem of liberalism. If you go back to the eighteenth century, Friedrich Schleiermacher, the great German liberal, tried to reach what he called "the cultured despisers of the gospel," but he came so close to them that he became like them. That's what liberalism has done ever since. Dean Inge said, "He who marries the spirit of the age soon becomes a widower." You speak to them, you become one with them, and then you join them.

The seeker-sensitive movement is a kind of evangelical recycling of liberalism when it makes the audience sovereign in that way. You can say of many of the seeker-sensitive sermons, "Where are the hard sayings of Christ? Where is the cost of discipleship? Where is the challenge to mortify the old person?" Those challenges are all gone, because an audience-pleasing gospel has taken over and in effect sold out the gospel, and all from the well-intentioned desire to reach people where they are.

How many of your people want simply to feel good rather than be challenged? That's the cultural context of today.

The Need for Reformation and Revival

The church of Jesus Christ needs to be a social reality truly shaped by theological cause, namely, the Word and Spirit of God. The church must let God be God, knowing that only when it lives and thrives by His truth and resources can it succeed. If the church makes anything else the principle of its existence, Christians risk living unauthorized lives of faith, exercising unauthorized ministries, and proclaiming an unauthorized gospel.

Those are sober words, but they get at what is at stake in modernity. The challenge is to let God be God, above the tools of modernity. And one part of that challenge is to let the church be the church. Pastors need to be content with the old-fashioned definitions of their "calling"—titles like "pastor," "preacher," "teacher," "the administrator of the sacraments," and so on—rather than defining themselves, as many of the modern leadership books do, by how well they delegate and facilitate. Those definitions are useful in their place, but not beyond their place. If they eat up the high calling of pastors, which is theological and spiritual, the church is in deep trouble.

As I said at the beginning of this chapter, pastors are the key to much of the hope for the church in the future. Yet many pastors are demoralized today; or, if they're not demoralized, they're truly in danger of pursuing the latest insights and technologies of modernity uncritically, which can eventually mean there is no need to let God be God. Instead, they should rest in the high demands of the biblical view of the calling of ministers and let the church be the church.

In a way, modernity is the world in which we live. We're called to be "in the world but not of the world." It's the most powerful culture in history. It's the world's first global culture, so it's the "world" as the New Testament uses that word—the cosmos over against our Lord—at its strongest and most pervasive. We have to face the question: What really is modernity? We have to see its blessings but also its dangers.

In a sense, we've created the illusion that God must not understand what's going on in the twentieth century. Some people put it blatantly—that on the Day of Pentecost, God used miraculous power because He didn't have (as one man put it) "our modern management [our modern marketing] technologies," which I think is utterly blasphemous.

There's an enormous crisis of religious authority in America.

Many evangelicals (in particular) see everything in we-they terms. "We" are fine, and "they" (secular humanists, New Agers, or the liberal elite) are the problem. But actually, the problem is far worse than that. "They" may be a problem, whoever "they" are. But the problem is as deeply in us, too. We can't comfort ourselves that it's all a matter of the culture wars and that once we overcome the opposition, we'll be fine, because the corruption is deep in the church of Christ, and it's deepest of all in evangelicalism.

In fact, today you could say that the wheel has come full circle. For 400 years, we believed that the prototype of scandal was that of the indulgence-selling Tetzel and the people Martin Luther so rightly attacked. But now the ultimate symbols of corruption are evangelical evangelists. And the televangelists are only the beginning of a deep corruption right across the face of evangelicalism. We are in deep disarray.

Now, there's nothing wrong with televangelists and the media per se. In fact, I think modernity is a magnificent opportunity for the gospel. It gives us—through things like radio, television, video tapes, audio tapes, the Internet, cable television, and satellite link-ups—opportunities to reach the entire world. Modern technologies are equivalent to the printing presses at the time of the Reformation, or to the Roman roads and the Greek language in the first century. They're an enormous opportunity that we must seize but use discerningly.

Alonzo McDonald contributed to a book I edited with John Seel called *No God But God: Breaking with the Idols of Our Age*. In that book, McDonald wrote, "Modern management can be the kiss of death if its approach overshadows rather than reinforces the basic mission" of the organization. Now, Al McDonald is not at all a simplistic, antimanagement person. He is one of the world's great management experts, a man of enormous experience and wisdom, having been the worldwide CEO of McKinsey & Company for 15 years.

McDonald points out, however, that one feature of human institutions is that they have an underlying idol—the idol of immortality, which shows itself in a desire to perpetuate themselves. One way this idol shows itself is when an institution's desire to sustain itself overcomes its original mission, and that original mission gets lost in just maintaining the institution with its short-term goals. When that happens, the institution actually has the seeds of its own destruction built into it.

The key thing, then, is for the institution to keep faithful to the original vision and make sure that all the techniques don't become a game in themselves, but that they serve the vision and keep the flame alive.

Conclusion: First Things

We need to remind ourselves that since Jesus Christ is true, the church is more than just another human institution. He alone is its Head. There are at least six simple but tough things needed to make sure we do not diminish His headship of His church:

1. *A radical confrontation with sin, heresy, worldliness, idolatry, and judgment.* These negative categories are virtually missing in evangelicalism today. But they're key issues, because the gospel says no to what's wrong before it says yes to what's right.

2. *A recovery of the forgotten first things of the gospel.* Many of the first things of the gospel are lost today, and no amount of modern insight and technology will ever make up for them.

3. *The revitalization of the laity.* An awful lot of lip service is given to this concept, but it is not actually happening in much of the world.

4. *The reintegration of truth and theology*. Evangelicals are no longer people of truth, and we need to go back to that, because it's absolutely fundamental to the faith as the Scriptures define it.

5. *A re-exertion of genuine leadership in evangelicalism.* We have a profound crisis of leadership, and many of our leaders don't have a

concern for all of the evangelical movement, but simply for their own ministries.

6. The recovery of the past. Many evangelicals have a huge blind spot between Revelation 22 and the year 1900. The whole past—the great men and women of Christian history—is lost to them, and that's a very dangerous loss.

When we put these things together, we see that we need to redefine evangelicalism today. Evangelicals are not just polyester-suited people or the Christian-right stereotypes. We are people who define ourselves by the first things of the gospel of Jesus Christ, and we have to live that gospel as well as proclaim it. And we need to go back to an evangelicalism that is truly redefined according to the Bible.

The church of Christ is more than spiritual and theological, but never less. Only when first things are truly first, over even the best and most attractive of second things, will the church be free of idols, free to let God be God, free to be itself, and free to experience the growth that matters.

How do we get our eyes off the attractive second things and put our eyes on what many seem to feel is kind of a mundane, boring life lived in the knowledge and understanding that God is God?

Many of the modern things seem, on the other hand, much more alluring and apparently attractive. But anyone who looks at the Scriptures or surveys history knows that in the long run, those things will prove disappointing. We need pastors who have the courage to go back to the first things of the gospel, who really have confidence in the spiritual and theological depth of their calling, and who will not be mesmerized by modernity.

Modernity will prove to be a broken reed. Not only that, but it will also prove to be an alluring and seductive idol. We don't reject modernity; we use it in its place. But we need pastors who have simple confidence in the sovereignty of God and the high calling of being those who speak of the gospel of Jesus Christ. We need pastors who put the first things first. As Richard John Neuhaus says, "The first thing to say about politics is that politics is not the first thing." That can be applied to many of the gifts of modernity. It's the first things of the gospel that matter in the long run.

Pastor *to* Pastor

Whew! A chapter from Os Guinness is certain to be heady! Let me bring it all home with a quotation from Dr. Dobson. In March 1993, he wrote, "What is needed are millions of believers [and thousands of pastors!] who will remain true to their convictions and ask God to help them prevail against overwhelming odds. The prize to the winner: our children and grandchildren."

As you sort through modernity and how—and to what degree—you can or can't use it in your ministry, remember that your decisions affect not just yourself and the adults in your church, but also the youth and children in your church. We must pass the faith on to them!

Here are some things that are clear:

- *We must take America back for Christ.*
- *We must find answers to why America is so violent and immoral.*
- *We must do all we can to stabilize the family and challenge the men of our nation to take up their mantle of leadership.*
- *We must continue to pray for a renewed and courageous church, knowing that prayer without action won't change things.*

There must be a time of national humiliation and repentance. And yes, we, America's pastors, must see ourselves as catalysts in taking back America.

We must hear the command of God to Joshua: "Do not be terrified; do not be discouraged, for the Lord *your God will be with you wherever you go" (Josh. 1:9).*

So, pastor, as you go out in our modern world to minister, know that the Lord who chose you to be a pastor (see John 15:16) is cheering for you (see Matt. 28:18-20) and promises never to forsake you.

H. B. L.

12

Don Bubna is a good and valued colleague. For nearly two decades, I had the privilege of pastoring with him in Salem, Oregon. We lived in a community that was almost like a Camelot for pastors. Although there was friendly competition among the churches, it was a great city in which to serve because we had similar dreams and burdens for our town. As clergy, we talked often, loved each other, and to my knowledge never took pride in the fact that our churches were succeeding at the expense of another. We talked openly about people "church hopping" and realized early on that if you live and grow on folks who jump from one church to the other, you will, in time, suffer at the hand of those same people.

I remember it well: In our city of many churches, there were five major so-called conservative churches and two mainline congregations who had a great deal of prominence. It was a unique mix but one that caught the attention of the entire community. We were all growing and reaping a harvest of souls until one day, for some reason, all but one of those churches suffered terribly because of unresolved internal conflict. Fortunately, I wasn't around when it all fell apart, but fall apart it did, and the pain for everyone has been immense. Don Bubna's church, to my knowledge, was the only congregation in the bunch to "dodge the bullet," but as he will relate to you vividly in this chapter, he didn't "dodge the bullet" in his next assignment. He is candid, transparent, and in no way vindictive, but as you read his words, you can't help but feel his suffering. He, like many of you, has survived to live another day. But as I recall a conversation we had shortly after the "blow" had landed, I'm not sure he knew at that time if he would make it. Thank God he did.

This probably doesn't come as any surprise to you, but did you realize contention in the local church is one reason people say they no longer attend? "Why would I go to church to find more conflict when there is so much in the everyday world?" they say.

One pastor's wife wrote me, "The problems and conflict in the church began to affect our marriage."

Another pastor said, "Every pastor I know of has someone or some small group within the church that has an ungodly attitude. I was never informed in seminary about these people or how to deal with them. I thought if I walked uprightly and with a pure heart and tried to get along, they would do the same. They didn't."

Please, pastor, read this chapter with an open mind, and allow yourself to have a very teachable spirit.

H. B. London Jr.

Dealing with Conflict in the Church

by Donald Bubna

"Conflict—particularly conflict between boards and pastors—is now an epidemic."

So says my friend Gerhard Du Toit, an evangelist who has extensive ministry experience throughout the U.S. and Canada, and I agree with him.

I am now a pastor-at-large in the Christian and Missionary Alliance, and in that capacity, I work with pastors and congregations across North America. Conflict is common to most. I've also had firsthand experience with conflict. I want to tell that story in the hope that what I learned will be of help to you, the reader. But first let me set the stage.

As a pastor, I served three churches (one in California, one in Oregon, and one in Canada) for a total of 38 years, and I had conflict in all three of those churches. In fact, having conflict is natural. It's human, and it's not unusual. What makes all the difference, though, is how we deal with it.

Further, the amount of conflict in our culture has intensified significantly. We distrust people in leadership much more than did previous generations. Watergate and the Vietnam War certainly added to that distrust and conflict, as did the moral and integrity problems of some television evangelists. Consequently, people are quick to question the motives of all leaders, maybe especially Christian leaders.

Therefore, it should come as no surprise that forcing out pastors is common today—far too common. My five years in Canada were the most exciting and in many ways the most fulfilling of my 38 years of ministry. But they ended with the greatest hurt I've known in the pastorate when I had to offer a resignation I did not initiate. It's not the way one wants to finish.

According to a special report in *Your Church* magazine (March/April 1996), one-third of all pastors (34%) serve congregations who either fired the previous minister or actively forced his or her resignation. Recently, *Alliance Life* reported that 2,500 pastors were forced to resign in one large denomination alone the year before. That number represents about 7 percent of the churches in that denomination. But that doesn't mean only 7 percent of the churches in that denomination were in conflict! It means the conflict between the pastor and the board or some other persons was so great in 2,500 of those churches that that many pastors resigned—in one year.

In many of the churches where terminations occur, there are numerous problems: Attendance is down; membership has fallen; finances are difficult. But in the last church I pastored, attendance had doubled during the five years of my ministry. The church's outreach was significant, and we had mothered a daughter congregation. No one denied that the church was having a major influence on the community. The problem that caused me to leave was not lack of growth, nor was it conflict with the denomination. From my perspective, the cause was a power struggle. And I think a power issue is at the heart of most church conflicts that cause a pastor to leave.

It's often a question of roles. Who really leads? Who's in charge?

Power. Control. Getting my way. This is what the world system is about. Assert yourself. Negotiate the best deal. Fulfillment comes by self-indulgence. That's our culture's message. And people don't come into the church without bringing some of that baggage.

Pastors aren't beyond the need for significance and the enjoyment of power, either. Meetings of the church board become the stage for our old nature to unveil itself. Who hasn't said things, especially at a late-night meeting, that he hasn't later regretted?

As Lyle Schaller has said, "Politics is always dirty play, but in the church it is at its worst." That's because in the church, we all have so much at stake: our traditions, our way of life, our income, our investment of funds, and our family. When any of those is threatened—or when people simply feel threatened—the conflict really becomes intense.

When I first came to the church from which I was asked to resign, the key question I was asked repeatedly was, "Can you be strong enough to lead this church with very strong people in it? Can you put together a strong staff and lead that staff?" My answer was, "I think I can," and for four years I was that strong leader. But then the founders of that church—which had been only 12 years old when I arrived and was only 17 years old when I left—felt their power being threatened.

One of them came to me six months before I left and said at lunch, "You've had five very good years here, and you ought to feel very good about that. We do," he continued, but then he added, "We change pastors every five years. Do you understand what I'm saying?"

He felt that he was no longer getting the time before the congregation and receiving their attention as he formerly had. He said it was wrong that he could no longer exercise his leadership gifts.

His family and friends became a part of his movement for change. The leadership of the church's governing board (numbering about 14) also changed, so that when I left, only 1 person remained who was in place when I had arrived. Ministry was going on in the church, and outreach was taking place. But the agenda had shifted.

Ray Ortlund

Let me tell you about my forced resignation. It came after I had been at Lake Avenue Congregational Church in California. I went from there to another California church—a fine church!— but I didn't fit.

Representatives from the church said to me, "You're living here; you've had all this experience; and we're in trouble. Won't you come and help us?"

I said, "I'm more of a traditional pastor. You're not a traditional church; you're a church of the '60s. You're kind of against building; you're kind of against worship services; you're against all these things." They knew a lot about what they were not going to be, and I came in with my background in all those things.

Nonetheless, Anne and I prayed and asked the Lord about it. It seemed to us, as we prayed, that God said, "Okay, do this." So I told the church, "I don't know if this will work, but I'll try to help you."

We got in there, and it was hard all the way! We faced rejection. I was working too hard, but my lead-

Each of us is capable of giving way to "self." Then the issue becomes preserving our self-esteem, values, and power position in the church, and that takes precedence over ministry. God is no longer in charge.

My faults in pastoring are a shame to me. I was often in too big a hurry. Impatience is a way of trying to usurp God's control. I lacked humility. I needed to listen more. I didn't read the signs. I could be defensive. We pastors are capable of doing dumb things.

Dealing with the Problem

How are we to deal with conflict in the church?

1. First, we must realize there's a cost to our calling. The Man we're following said to us, "Come after Me, take up your cross, and follow Me." To sense that we and our work are rejected is not fun. But our Savior was "despised and rejected of men." It can come from the people in religious power. We ought not to be so surprised. Suffering, sacrifice, and submission are what ministry is about. Ask Paul. Or read 2 Corinthians again for the first time. Look at the lives of the men and women of God through the ages. A. W. Tozer said it well: "The man God chooses to use, He must hurt him very deeply first."

So suffering is part of our calling. These trials become God's tools to develop us in godliness.

2. Second, develop a prayer ministry with leaders. My practice has always been to ask for the board and staff to meet weekly for worship, prayer, and discipling. Tuesday mornings early worked well, with an optional breakfast following. Rarely have I ever had conflict with a person that wasn't readily resolved if we freely participated in this together. Likewise, each regular monthly meeting of the board was started with worship, prayer, and some mutual caring. I developed short, serendipity Bible exercises to facilitate these events. Only on an occasion or two did I hear complaints about this approach to meetings.

3. Third, prepare your church for conflict through a solid teaching of the Word of God. Help people see that conflict occurred in the early church. It can be seen in all of Paul's letters, which were written to correct problems. Teach your church that if conflict happened in the early church, it will also happen in our congregation at some time.

Teach also the procedure Jesus gave us for handling conflict. Matthew 18:15-18 tells us that the way to begin is to go to the offending parties and speak to them. We tend to talk *about* people; that's gossip. In the church, we're supposed to speak to the people themselves. If they don't hear us when we go individually, then according to Jesus' teaching, we take a second person. If they still don't hear us, we go to the church, which may be the

ership still was not accepted. Nothing I could do was right. The church had suffered a split; so they were leery of their former pastor, and they were leery of me.

To make a long story short, I was asked to resign.

Now, one of the keys to dealing with the emotions involved in that whole situation came about through my wife's and my reading of the Bible. We read through the Bible together every year, and we had just finished Job. I said to Anne, "I noticed that when Job prayed for his friends, God changed his fortunes and restored him. We're going to pray for this church every day—not that God will bring calamity on them, shape them, or teach them anything. We're just going to pray God's blessing on their heads."

More than a decade later, we still do that every night when we pray. We ask for that church to be blessed of God. And they are. They're doing wonderfully. They've never been in better shape. And it kept us from bitterness. We love them.

I think God helped us when we determined to discipline ourselves to pray blessing on them. You see, I had found myself full of anger, and I had to admit that anger to the Lord and pray against it. I found myself full of fear and self-doubt, because my ministry had been rejected, and I felt like a terrible failure. I had a poor view of myself as a pastor and a preacher. It was the pits!

I would say to you pastors—and your wives—who are going through something like what we went through, "Oh brothers and sisters! This is a hard time. Remember that even though that church did not appreciate your ministry, you're still loved of God, and God still has a future for you. It doesn't do any good to put yourself down. But pray for those who persecute you; pray for those who misuse you. Then remember to put your head up and go into the future God has planned for you."

governing board or the whole congregation, according to the case.

All leaders need to model this procedure in the church. But few churches practice it or even take Jesus' words seriously. So rather than becoming a positive experience, conflict is devastating to the people who are attacked and destructive to the church body. Board members shouldn't even listen to rumors about church leaders unless there are two or three witnesses. Thus said Paul in 1 Timothy 5:19. Boards and pastors would do well to study Matthew 18:15-18 and 1 Timothy 5:17-20 together. Excellent material on this is available from the Institute for Christian Conciliation, 1537 Avenue D, Suite 352, Billings, MT 59102.

4. Fourth, see conflict as something God can use for good. If it's not a big issue, we need to stretch a bit more and overlook the offense.

If it is significant, we need to examine ourselves and get the beams out of our own eyes. Humbling ourselves before God is always positive. Without some conflict, we tend to forget this discipline.

When we need to approach someone else, we must do it in "meekness and lowliness," looking after others' interests more than our own. This produces Christlikeness in us.

We need also to focus on our contribution to the problem—to repent before God and make things right with people.

As the local church begins to practice

biblical peacemaking, little is said publicly. But such accountability leads to maturity, and God is glorified in His church.

5. *Finally, recognize when, in God's sovereignty, it's time for you to leave a church.* There's going to come a time when new leadership can serve the church better and your staying will only emphasize the problem and maybe split the church.

In my own situation, while by other people's estimates the complainers represented maybe 5 percent of the church—certainly no more than 10 percent—they influenced the board to the extent that I no longer had the support I needed. The honorable and godly thing to do was to comply with their request and submit to God's sovereignty.

But Leaving Isn't Easy

I wasn't raised in a parsonage, but my wife was, and she had never been through anything that hurt her as deeply as the conflict and our leaving that church. As pained as we were, though, we knew leaving and seeking some healing in our lives was the right thing to do. We had to try to forgive what we thought had been done to us and go on from there.

When, for the betterment of the church and our own emotional well-being, we conclude that it's necessary to leave a pastorate, it's not just a matter of losing a job or leaving one position to go to another. There's much more involved. A pastor told me recently that in being forced out of his pastorate, he lost his job, his home church, his self-esteem, and his community. He had to begin all over, and it was the most devastating event of his whole life. His children couldn't understand it, and they were crushed as well.

When a church forces a pastor to resign, the people doing the forcing often don't understand what the pastor and his family have to go through. When I was leaving my last church, I said at my final board meeting, "Do you realize, men, that in this move we will be losing 80 percent of our friends? I can't have contact with them anymore."

One of the men said, "I never thought of that."

But it was absolutely true.

Most board members look at it like a business decision. They think, *The church isn't growing fast enough, we don't like his leadership style, or we don't like his personality.* So then they think, *It's time to make a change, just as I would do in my business.*

A long-time chairman of the board and CEO of the J. C. Penney Company and a current vice president of Caterpillar International, both of whom have long been active churchmen, have both expressed their concern about this to me. They've witnessed too many pastor bashings and forced terminations that lacked integrity, and they insist that the business community treats its leaders with more kindness and grace than does the church.

But what happens *in* us is more important than what happens *to* us. Remember that Joseph's brothers didn't like his leadership style, either. They rejected him, sold him into slavery, and covered it all up with lies. They didn't know their treacherous act would be used by God to provide a haven for them all in a coming famine. But Joseph could say at that later date, "You meant it for evil, but God meant it for good."

Some Preventive Medicine

There's no way to conflict-proof your ministry. But there is a safe way to move on toward the fulfillment of your dreams in a particular church.

Before accepting a call, talk with your predecessor. Be aware of the weaknesses of the church leadership. Talk them out. Ask the board, "What might you do differently in transitioning a pastor out?"

Seek to clarify the role of the board and that of the pastor. Try to get this in writing.

Then work with your leaders. Make time with them a priority. "Dream the dream together." Agree on the vision for the church. Then articulate that vision with purposeful redundancy to the congregation.

Try to work with a governing board that is in the range of 8 to 10 men rather 12, 15, or more. Board meetings will be shorter and less tense, and the process of decision making will be simpler.

Consult weekly with two or three of the board members so that all decisions of any consequence are run through them. My rule of thumb is this: Get consensus from your staff and the executive committee of your board before anything is brought to the board itself.

Do these things and you can avoid much conflict.

Staffs: The Second-Greatest Area of Conflict

The second-greatest area of conflict in churches is between the senior pastor and his staff. My greatest joys and deepest pains have come through fellow staff members. They often contribute to disputes between a pastor and his board because people from the board or the congregation will try to drive a wedge between the senior pastor and the staff. So if you have a multiple staff, follow Bill Hybels's advice. He says three qualities are required of every staff member: godliness, competence in his or her area, and loyalty to the senior pastor.

Godliness takes time. Competence is something you can help a person develop. But if a person isn't loyal, you can't help him. So the moment a staff member can no longer support the senior pastor, that person should leave. He should leave right away—that week if possible. He needs to find a place where he can be loyal to the senior pastor.

Statistics show that the average associate will stay less than two years in any one place. It's easy for a senior pastor arriving at a new church and inheriting its staff to want to be nice and keep the whole team. It's best, though, to present them with Hybels's criteria and say to each one, "Let's take a few months to look at one another. Then if you or I feel you're going to be happier and more effective somewhere else, let's say so. That way, we'll be acting for the long-term good of the whole church."

Try to stay close to your staff. It's not bad to try to be familylike with staff members. Root for one another, and try to enhance each person's ministry. When one member is down, the others should try to help pick him up.

Certainly you can be hurt in such relationships. But as a staff, we have to be a microcosm of what we want the church to be. We must model authentic, caring relationship for the congregation. That calls for vulnerability. And when we do it, we're going to get walked on at some point. It may be a long time before that happens, but it will happen. To love is to risk. The alternative is not to love and to become a person who is mentally ill.

Help for When the Hard Time Hits You

When the going gets tough, materials like this book can be of help. In addition, some denominations are putting reconciliation committees into effect. My own denomination is now organizing such a committee in our district in Canada. I wish it had been in place before I went through the conflict at our church! The Mennonite church has assembled a number of reconciliation committees that will help not just churches in struggles, but individuals within churches as well. I encourage you to seek that kind of help. The Institute for Christian Conciliation, mentioned earlier, is available by phone at 406-256-1583, and Ken Sande, its director, has written a helpful book called *The Peacemaker*.

Also, when the devastating time came for me, for some weeks I received several calls a day from people around Canada and the U.S. offering prayer support. This surprise affirmation was very healing. If you know men and women who are going through transitions, get on the phone or write and affirm them. Let them know you care.

Finally, here are five key habits to practice when the hard time of conflict comes:

1. *Submit to God's sovereignty.* I can't understand why He allows all these conflicts to occur, but I know He does allow them, and He causes them to work for good. In my case, He used the situation to refine my life. I had some rough edges that needed to be knocked off. He also prepared me to help people in ways I had never imagined before. I write and speak with new compassion and understanding. Pastors and boards listen with high interest when they know you, too, have suffered.

2. *Find someone to be accountable to.* Maybe you'll need several people. When I was going through my difficult time, a friend named Arnold

Cook wrote me a note in which he asked three questions: "Are you leaving at peace with all men as much as depends on you? Is there anyone you've not forgiven? How has this affected your marriage, your thought life, and your confidence in the church?" I needed to answer them honestly. I need accountability, as do we all.

3. *Confess your faults.* Take responsibility for your shortcomings. Make things right with God and others. Let go of your anger. Do all you can to be reconciled to one another. Understand that some people won't be ready for this. Wait. You can't go further in rebuilding relationships than they will allow.

4. *Learn to forgive.* Forgiveness is a process, like grief. I have forgiven; but then something happens, the anger boils up inside me, and I have to acknowledge it's real anger. I have to choose to forgive again, get past the anger, and understand that the memories will keep resurfacing. So—like God—I need to keep on forgiving. When I don't forgive, I put myself in prison.

5. *Be an instrument of peace.* When Christ said, "Blessed are the peacemakers," He referred to those who actively pursue peace by how they live—in the ways they react and relate to people they meet along the way. Pursue peace in your own situation. Also, reach out and help a brother where you're not a part of the problem. Consider this quotation from *Peacemaking, the Quiet Power*:

> The Christian church has been in existence for several thousand years now. In its history there have been innumerable fights and conflicts and battles, and yet, the church has survived. This certainly gives credence and evidence of the Holy Spirit of Christ and His power to mediate when we have differences. But the intensity and frequency of conflict have become increasingly more apparent in the last two decades. The reasons? Well, they are many and varied. Furthermore, these reasons

> certainly mirror the changes in our society as a whole. Mediation can give greater stability and more hope to the church in our complex time. The Holy Spirit of Christ has so many ways of working. We're living in a time when this Holy Spirit is ready to take the means and vehicles of grace that Christ continually offers and show them to us. We are vehicles through which the Holy Spirit can work. Mediation is a vehicle in which the Holy Spirit can create, through us, the process of keeping peace. The goal is peacemaking, and it is Christ our Lord who towers over all of us, the one true Mediator, the Prince of Peace.

Finally, to have conflict is human; to respond with grace is divine. In our fallen nature, we will experience pain in relationships. Usually, at least in part, it will be of our own making. As we respond with grace, we allow God to work further in us. He is glorified. The church is edified. And the world again witnesses that in all our differences, we truly love one another.

Pastor *to* Pastor

Question: Is there someone in your church with whom you're experiencing conflict? Is there more than one person? Take some time right now and pray for that person or those people.

Now, stop and examine yourself in God's presence. Have you been in the wrong in any way? How have you contributed to the conflict with the person or people you just prayed for? Would it be helpful if you would take the initiative and attempt to make things right with them? Stop again and pray for guidance from our loving Lord, who cares about you and those you serve and is at work to bring good out of even these conflicts. Thank Him that you can trust He is at work.

In a baseball game, someone has to lose. Few sports allow for a game to go into the record books as a tie. But in the Christian life, none of us has to be a loser. And that includes you, my friend.

None of us are losers—although we often feel the pain of the battle. We give it our best and take our lumps, and sometimes, when we look up at the scoreboard, we see results that truly seem to be negative. But though that may be true in man's eyes, it's not true in God's.

I receive a lot of letters from pastors ready to toss in the towel simply because they've lost a few—or thought they did! No way! "If God is for us, who can be against us? . . . We are more than conquerors through him who loved us" (Rom. 8:31, 37).

You are a winner, my friend. A winner! Don't ever quit! Don't ever give up, regardless of the apparent score!

H. B. L.

13

Francis Schaeffer affected my life as a young pastor in ways that are still bearing fruit. It began with his book Whatever Happened to the Human Race? *and subsequent film series entitled "How Should We Then Live?" He was a man before his time because he talked and wrote about things no one else did. In his book, he opened the door to the possibility that in time, our society would come to accept such things as abortion, infanticide, euthanasia, child abuse, and the like. I remember sitting spellbound in a sanctuary filled with people as we watched his film series and we gasped and uttered under our breath, "Oh, that could never happen in our country. No way!" But it has.*

I also remember feeling his great love for pastors and their families as, in his empathetic, solid, almost monotone voice, he would challenge the church and those who led her to be watchful and vigilant. He would warn that we not find ourselves blindsided by society and humanism. To be honest, Francis Schaeffer was too deep for me most of the time, but every now and again I would "get it," and my life was different. He wrote,

> *If we ache and have compassion for humanity today in our own country and across the world, we must do all that we can to help people see the truth of Christianity and accept Christ as Savior. And we must stand against the loss of humanness in all its forms. . . . In the end we must realize that the tide of humanism, with its loss of humanness, is not merely a cultural ill, but a spiritual ill that the truth given us in the Bible and Christ alone can cure. (*Whatever Happened to the Human Race?*)*

This chapter is for those of you who might be struggling with who you are and where you are. That's okay—in fact, it's normal, but not if it steals your joy and, in time, renders you ineffective for the cause of Christ and the people you serve.

In our book The Heart of a Great Pastor *(p. 72), Neil Wiseman and I wrote,*

> *Ministry never bursts into full bloom at a magic moment in the future when one has more experience, finds the right town or receives some favored advantage. Effective ministry does not start in the misty distance. Your current post has a wealth of hidden potential. Why not find it?*
>
> *Now is a good time to push through the fog of frustration or self-doubt to a new beginning. Stop waiting and start blooming where God has planted you. Realize that a second or third or fourth beginning for ministry can be more exhilarating, more fulfilling and more realistic than the first.*
>
> *Today is all we have, but today is enough.*

Oh, I know words are cheap, and you can easily say to me, "H. B., you just don't understand. It's really tough out here." But one thing I can say with certainty is that God knows, and He cares. He even understands. I beg you to treasure the present and use it well. See yourself as "wood in God's house," and as Neil and I say, "Cultivate your spirituality, stability and strength to bloom a supernatural ministry in your present assignment."

H. B. London Jr.

No Little People, No Little Places

by Francis Schaeffer

One thing that has encouraged me is the way God used Moses' rod, a stick of wood. Many years ago, when I was a young pastor just out of seminary, a study of the use of Moses' rod, which I called "God So Used a Stick of Wood," was a crucial factor in giving me the courage to press on.

The story of Moses' rod began when God spoke to Moses from the burning bush, telling him to go and challenge Egypt, the greatest power of his day. Moses reacted, "Who am I, that I should go unto Pharaoh, and that I should bring forth the children of Israel out of Egypt?" (Exod. 3:11, KJV). God directed Moses' attention to the simplest thing imaginable—the staff in his own hand, a shepherd's rod, a stick of wood. But when Moses obeyed God's command to toss it to the ground, it became a serpent, and Moses himself fled from it. God next ordered him to take it by the tail, and when he did so, it became a rod again. Then God told him to go and confront the power of Egypt and meet Pharaoh face to face with this rod in his hand.

Exodus 4:20 tells us the secret of all that followed: The rod of Moses had become the rod of God.

Standing in front of Pharaoh, Aaron cast down this rod, and it became a serpent. As God spoke to Moses and as Aaron was the spokesman of Moses (see Exod. 4:16), so it would seem that Aaron used the rod of Moses which had become the rod of God. The wizards of Egypt, performing real magic through the power of the devil (not just a stage trick through sleight of hand), matched this. Here was demonic power. But the rod of God swallowed up the other rods. This was not merely a victory of Moses over Pharaoh, but of Moses' God over Pharaoh's god and the power of the devil behind that god.

This rod appeared frequently in ensuing events. The rod of God, indeed, was in Aaron's hand (see Exod. 7:17, 19, 20), and water was purified, an amazing use for a mere stick of wood. In the days that followed, Moses "stretched forth his rod," and successive plagues came upon the land (see Exod. 8:1–10:15). Watch the destruction of judgment that came from a dead stick of wood that had become the rod of God.

Pharaoh's grip on the Hebrews was shaken loose, and he let the people go. But then he changed his mind and ordered his armies to pursue them. When the armies came upon them, the Hebrews were caught in a narrow place, with mountains on one side of them and the sea on the other. And God said to Moses, "Lift up thy rod" (Exod. 14:16, KJV). Up to this point, the rod had been used for judgment and destruction, but now it was as much a rod of healing for the Jews as it had been a rod of judgment for the Egyptians. That which is in the hand of God can be used either way.

Later, the rod of judgment also became a rod of supply. In Rephidim, the people desperately needed water.

It must have been an amazing sight to stand before a great rock (not a small pebble, but a face of rock such as we see here in Switzerland in the mountains) and to see a rod struck against it, and then to watch torrents of life-giving water flow out to satisfy thousands of people and their livestock. The giver of judgment became the giver of life. It was not magic. There was nothing in the rod itself. The rod of Moses had simply become the rod of God. We, too, are not only to speak a word of judgment to our lost world, but are also to be a source of life as well.

The rod also brought military victory as it was held up (see Exod. 17:9). In a much later incident, the people revolted against Moses, and a test was established to see whom God had, indeed, chosen. The rod was placed before God, and it budded (see Num. 17:8). Incidentally, we find out what kind of tree it had come from so long ago because it now brought forth almond blossoms.

The final use of the rod occurred when the wilderness wandering was almost over. Forty years had passed since the people had left Egypt, so the rod may have been almost 80 years old. The people again needed water, and though they were now in a different place, the desert of Zin, they were still murmuring against God.

Moses took the rod (which verse 9 with 17:10 shows was the same one that had been kept with the ark since it had budded), and he struck the rock twice. He should have done what God had told him and only spoken with the rod in his hand, but that's another study. In spite of this, however, "water came out abundantly" (Num. 20:11, KJV).

Consider the mighty ways in which God used a dead stick of wood. "God so used a stick of wood" can be a banner cry for each of us. Though we are limited and weak in talent, physical energy, and psychological strength, we are not less than a stick of wood. But as the rod of Moses had to become the rod of God, so that which is me must become the me of God. Then I can become useful in God's hands. The Scripture emphasizes that much can come from little if the little is truly consecrated to God. There are no little people and no big people in the true spiritual sense, but only consecrated and unconsecrated people. The problem for each of us is applying this truth to ourselves: Is Francis Schaeffer the Francis Schaeffer of God?

H. B. London Jr.

Whatever stage of a pastor's life you're in, bloom where you're planted. Don't regret it. Don't find fault with it. Don't be obsessed with going to another stage. See what God will do for you where you are. Let Him use your gifts and abilities to His glory, and I'll guarantee you, one day, some time, some place—just as surely as you're reading these words—you'll look back on this passage in your ministry and say, "Thank You, God. Thank You for giving me the courage. Thank You for giving me the patience. Thank You that I didn't quit."

No Little Places

But if a Christian is consecrated, does that mean he will be in a big place instead of a little place? The answer, the next step, is very important: As there are no little people in God's sight, so there are no little places. To be wholly committed to God in the place where God wants him—this is the creature glorified. In my writing and lecturing, I put much emphasis on God's being the infinite reference point that integrates the intellectual problems of life. He is to be this, but He must be the reference point not only in our thinking, but also in our living. This means being what He wants me to be, where He wants me to be.

Nowhere more than in America are Christians caught in the twentieth-century syndrome of size. Size will show success. If I am consecrated, there will necessarily be large quantities of people, dollars, and so on. This is not so. Not only does God not say that size and spiritual power go together, but He even reverses this (especially in the teaching of Jesus) and tells us to be deliberately careful not to choose a place too big for us. We all tend to emphasize big works and big places, but all such emphasis is of the flesh. To think in such terms is simply to hearken back to the old, unconverted, egoist, self-centered Me. This attitude, taken from the world, is more dangerous to the Christian than fleshly amusement or practice. It is the flesh.

People in the world naturally want to boss

others. Imagine a boy beginning work with a firm. He has a lowly place and is ordered around by everyone: Do this! Do that! Every dirty job is his. He is the last man on the totem pole, merely one of Rabbit's friends-and-relations, in Christopher Robin's terms. So one day when the boss is out, he enters the boss's office, looks around carefully to see that no one is there, and then sits down in the boss's big chair. "Someday," he says, "I'll say 'run' and they'll run." This is man. And let us say with tears that a person does not automatically abandon this mentality when he becomes a Christian. In every one of us there remains a seed of wanting to be boss, of wanting to be in control and have the word of power over our fellows.

But the Word of God teaches us that we are to have a very different mentality:

> But Jesus called them [His disciples] to him, and saith unto them, Ye know that they who are accounted to rule over the Gentiles lord it over them; and their great ones exercise authority upon them. But so shall it not be among you; but whosoever will be great among you, shall be your minister; and whosoever of you will be the chiefest, shall be servant of all. For even the Son of Man came, not to be ministered unto but to minister, and to give his life a ransom for many. (Mark 10:42-45, KJV)

Every Christian, without exception, is called into the place where Jesus stood. To the extent that we are called to leadership, we are called to ministry, even costly ministry. The greater the leadership, the greater is to be the ministry. The word *minister* is not a title of power, but a designation of servanthood. There is to be no Christian guru. We must reject this constantly and carefully. A minister, a man who is a leader in the church of God (and never more needed than in a day like ours when the battle is so great), must make plain to the men, women, boys, and girls who come to places of leadership that instead of lording their authority over others and allowing it to become an ego trip, they are to serve in humility.

Again, Jesus said, "But be not ye called Rabbi; for one is your Master, even Christ, and all ye are brethren" (Matt. 23:8, KJV). This does not mean there is to be no order in the church. It does mean that the basic relationship between Christians is not that of elder and people, or pastor and people, but that of brothers and sisters in Christ. This denotes there is one Father in the family and that His offspring are equal. There are different jobs to be done, different offices to be filled, but we as Christians are equal before one Master. We are not to seek a great title; we are to have the places together as brethren.

When Jesus said, "He that is greatest among you shall be your servant" (Matt. 23:11, KJV), He was not speaking in hyperbole or uttering a romantic idiom. Jesus Christ is the realist of all realists, and when He says this to us, He is telling us something specific we are to do.

Our attitude toward all men should be that of equality, because we are common creatures. We are of one blood and kind. As I look across all the world, I must see every man as a fellow-creature, and I must be careful to have a sense of our equality on the basis of this common status. We must be careful in our thinking not to try to stand in the place of God to other men. We are fellow-creatures. And when I step from the creature-to-creature relationship into the brothers-and-sisters-in-Christ relationship within the church, how much more important to be a brother or sister to all who have the same Father. Orthodoxy, to a Bible-believing Christian, always has two faces. It has a creedal face and a practicing face, and Christ emphasizes that that is to be the case here. Dead orthodoxy is always a contradiction in terms, and clearly that is so here; to be a Bible-believing Christian demands humility regarding others in the Body of Christ.

Jesus gave us a tremendous example:

> Jesus knowing that the Father had given all things into his hands, and that he was come from God, and went to God; he riseth from supper, and laid aside his garments, and took a towel, and girded himself. After that he poureth water into a basin, and began to wash the disciples' feet, and to wipe them with the

> towel with which he was girded. . . . Ye call me Master and Lord; and ye say well; for so I am. If I, then, your Lord and Master, have washed your feet, ye also ought to wash one another's feet. For I have given you an example, that ye should do as I have done to you. Verily, verily, I say unto you, The servant is not greater than his lord; neither he that is sent greater than he that sent him. If ye know these things, happy are ye if ye do them. (John 13:3-5, 13-17, KJV)

Note that Jesus says that if we do these things, there will be happiness. It is not just knowing these things that brings happiness; it is doing them. Throughout Jesus' teaching, these two words *know* and *do* occur constantly and always in that order. We cannot do until we know, but we can know without doing. The house built on the rock is the house of the man who knows and does. The house built on the sand is the house of the man who knows but does not do.

Christ washed the disciples' feet and dried them with the towel with which He was girded—that is, with His own clothing. He intended this to be a practical example of the mentality and action that should be seen in the midst of the people of God.

Taking the Lowest Place

Yet another statement of Jesus bears on our discussion:

> And he put forth a parable to those who were bidden, when he marked how they chose out the chief rooms; saying unto them, When thou art bidden of any man to a wedding, sit not down in the highest room; lest a more honorable man than thou be bidden of him; and he that bade thee and him come and say to thee, Give this man place; and thou begin with shame to take the lowest room. But when thou art bidden, go and sit down in the lowest room that, when he that bade thee cometh, he may say unto thee, Friend, go up higher; then shalt thou have worship in

> the presence of them that sit at meat with thee. For whosoever exalteth himself shall be abased; and he that humbleth himself shall be exalted. (Luke 14:7-11, KJV)

Jesus commands Christians to seek consciously the lowest position. All of us—pastors, teachers, professional religious workers, and nonprofessional included—are tempted to say, "I will take the larger place because it will give me more influence for Jesus Christ." Both individual Christians and Christian organizations fall prey to the temptation of rationalizing this way as we build bigger and bigger empires. But according to the Scripture, this is backward: We should consciously take the lowest place unless the Lord Himself extrudes us into a greater one.

The word *extrude* is important here. To be extruded is to be forced out under pressure into a desired shape. Picture a huge press jamming soft metal at high pressure through a die, so that the metal comes out in a certain shape. This is the way of the Christian: He should choose the lesser place until God extrudes him into a position of more responsibility and authority.

Let me suggest two reasons why we ought not grasp the larger place. First, we should seek the lowest place because there it is easier to be quiet before the face of the Lord. I did not say *easy*; in no place, no matter how small or humble, is it easy to be quiet before God. But it is certainly easier in some places than in others. And the little places, where I can more easily be close to God, should be my preference. I am not saying that it is impossible to be quiet before God in a greater place, but God must be allowed to choose when a Christian is ready to be extruded into such a place, for only He knows when a person will be able to have some quietness before Him in the midst of increased pressure and responsibility.

Quietness and peace before God are more important than any influence a position may seem to give, for we must stay in step with God to have the power of the Holy Spirit. If by taking a bigger place our quietness with God is lost, then to that extent our fellowship with Him is broken and we are living in the flesh, and the final result will not be as great, no matter how important the larger place may look in the eyes of other men or in our own eyes. Always there will be a battle, always we will be less than perfect, but if a place is too big and too active for our present spiritual condition, then it is too big.

We see this happen over and over again, and perhaps it has happened at some time to us: Someone whom God has been using marvelously in a certain place takes it upon himself to move into a larger place and loses his quietness with God. Ten years later, he may have a huge organization, but the power has gone, and he is no longer a real part of the battle in his generation. The final result of not being quiet before God is that less will be done, not more—no matter how much Christendom may be beating its drums or playing its trumpets for a particular activity.

So we must not go out beyond our depth. Take the smaller place so you have quietness before God. I am not talking about laziness; let me make that clear. That is something else, something, too, which God hates. I am not talking about copping out or dropping out. God's people are to be active, not seeking, on account of some false mystical concept, to sit constantly in the shade of the rock. There is no monasticism in Christianity. We will not be lazy in our relationship with God, because when the Holy Spirit burns, a man is consumed. We can expect to become physically tired in the midst of battle for our King and Lord; we should not expect all of life to be a vacation. We are talking about quietness before God as we are in His place for us. The size of the place is not important, but the consecration in that place is.

It must be noted that all these things which are true for an individual are true also for a group. A group can become activistic and take on responsibilities God has not laid upon it. For both the individual and the group, the first reason we are not to grasp (and the emphasis is on *grasp*) the larger place is that we must not lose our quietness with God.

The second reason we should not seek the larger place is that if we deliberately and egotistically lay hold on leadership, wanting the drums to beat and the trumpets to blow, then we are not qualified for leadership. Why? Because we have forgotten that we are brothers and sisters in

Christ with other Christians. I have said on occasion that there is only one good kind of fighter for Jesus Christ—the man who does not like to fight. The belligerent man is never the one to be belligerent for Jesus. And it is exactly the same with leadership. The Christian leader should be a quiet man of God who is extruded by God's grace into some place of leadership.

We all have egoistic pressures inside us. We may have substantial victories over them, and we may grow, but we never completely escape them in this life. The pressure is always there deep in my heart and soul, needing to be faced with honesty. These pressures are evident in the smallest of things as well as the greatest. I have seen fights over who was going to be the president of a Sunday school class composed of three members. The temptation has nothing to do with size. It comes from a spirit, a mentality, inside us. The person in leadership for leadership's sake is returning to the way of the world, like the boy dusting off the boss's chair and saying, "Someday I'll sit in it, and I'll make people jump."

One of the loveliest incidents in the early church occurred when Barnabas concluded that Paul was the man of the hour and then had to seek him out because Paul had gone back to Tarsus, his own little place. Paul was not up there nominating himself; he was back in Tarsus, even out of communication as far as we can tell. When Paul called himself "the chief of sinners...not meet to be an apostle" (1 Tim. 1:15; 1 Cor. 15:9, KJV), he was not speaking just for outward form's sake. From what he said elsewhere and from his actions, we can see that this was Paul's mentality. Paul, the man of leadership for the whole Gentile world, was perfectly willing to be in Tarsus until God said to him, "This is the moment."

Being a Rod of God

The people who receive praise from the Lord Jesus will not in every case be the people who hold leadership in this life. There will be many persons who were sticks of wood that stayed close to God and were quiet before Him, and were used in power by Him in a place that looks small to men.

Each Christian is to be a rod of God in the place of God for him. We must remember throughout our lives that in God's sight, there are no little people and no little places. Only one thing is important: to be consecrated persons in God's place for us, at each moment. Those who think of themselves as little people in little places, if committed to Christ and living under His lordship in the whole of life, may, by God's grace, change the flow of our generation. And as we get on a bit in our lives, knowing how weak we are, if we look back and see we have been somewhat used of God, then we should be the rod "surprised by joy."

Pastor *to* Pastor

The late Dr. Schaeffer wrote, "Consider the mighty ways in which God used a dead stick of wood." His point: There are no little people. Then he said, "Not only does God not say that size and spiritual power go together, but He even reverses this (especially in the teaching of Jesus) and tells us to be deliberately careful not to choose a place too big for us." His point: There are no little places. He concluded: "Only one thing is important: to be consecrated persons in God's place for us, at each moment."

My friend, are you seeking to be somebody? Don't strive—you already are somebody, because God chose you, loves you, and clothes you in Christ's own righteousness. When people look your way, they see someone they respect and admire, not because of your ability to speak or teach, or even because you're a pastor, but because—in Christ—you're a good person who loves God, his family, and his fellow man.

The Bible says that Noah "was a righteous man, blameless among the people of his time, and he walked with God" (Gen. 6:9). Noah was a real hero—a hero of the faith! And you are, too!

Maybe you should have your computer print out a banner that you can hang on the wall opposite the desk in your study that will say: "No Little People, No Little Places!"

Remember, if the Lord wants you to be a Paul, He'll make you to be a Paul; otherwise, be content to be who He created you to be. And if the Lord wants to put you into a church with 10,000 members, He'll bring them in—and prepare you to pastor them. Trust Him to keep you where you are until He shows you it's time to move somewhere else.

You are somebody! God created you and regenerated you. You are His adopted son. Please don't forget it, and press on for His "Well done." Finish strong!

H. B. L.

Epilogue

by H. B. London Jr.

Thank you for taking the time to read *Refresh, Renew, Revive*. Haven't you been blessed by the insights and encouragement of our colleagues in the ministry? We're endebted to all of them for allowing us a peek into their hearts and the chance to walk a bit of their journey with them. They weren't chosen because of their "celebrity" but because of their concern and their genuine love for folks like you who do what they do—and have done. Now, as we conclude this book, let me share one last thought with you.

Sometimes in my lonely, quiet moments, I wonder if I've done all I've done the way God had in mind for me. I hark back to the little church on the "wrong side of the tracks" where I began pastoring in 1963 as a young man just out of seminary. Nobody wanted to go minister there. Nobody wanted to be there.

I received the invitation to pastor that little church while I was in seminary in Kansas City. I didn't know anything about it. I took it on faith and made the huge sum of $50 a week. We didn't have a parsonage, and I commuted 30 miles each way for 3 or 4 months before we ever found a place to live. But I'm telling you now, as I look back at that experience, that there was probably no better time in my life. I learned so much! Beverley and I discovered what ministry was about, and in many ways I determined the philosophy of ministry that would guide me for a lifetime.

The journey continued as I went to the next church in a steel-mill town with a bunch of rough, tough guys. But it was there that I came to understand how important ministry to men was, and that if I could win the man to Jesus Christ, the family would follow nearly 100 percent of the time.

From there, I went to a traditional church in the state of Oregon, where I served for 18 years. When I arrived, the church was stuck in a rut. I remember sitting at a board meeting and saying to the men there—and bear in mind that I was only 29 years old—"You know, this isn't working. I came here because I thought God had given me a vision and a dream for this place, but it's not working." I begged them, "If you men will give me 6 months and let me dream my dreams and see what God can do with this place, and if at the end of 6 months it's not working, I'll leave without a whimper. I'll go back to California."

And you know what? They heard me. Everyone on the board looked toward the leader, and he said, "Well, let's give the young man a chance." That decision was followed by 18 wonderful, productive, Camelot years!

In 1985, I went to Southern California, where I faced the almost unimaginable task of following a gifted pastor who had been in the church for 19 years. I also inherited a debt of $6.5 million. The building payments alone were staggering. Besides, I was mourning the loss of a church where I had been for so long and coming into a situation where I wanted the people to love me the way they loved the pastor who had been with them for nearly 2 decades. It was tough!

For a year and a half there, I was my own worst enemy and literally found myself sitting up at night, watching the TV test pattern, because I was so confused about what God was doing and how unhappy I was. But then, all of a sudden, something snapped me back to reality. The whole idea of blooming where I was planted began to make sense. Ministry would not be a cakewalk, and life might not be fair—all those things quickly came into focus, and I began to realize God had me where I was for that season of my life and ministry. So I gave it my best, and God blessed.

Meanwhile, during conversations with Jim Dobson on Friday evenings, when we'd go out and eat together once or twice a month, and on Sunday nights when, after church, we'd collapse from the week and try to recoup, the whole idea of a ministry to pastors through Focus on the Family emerged. That was 1991.

Do I miss pastoring? More than I can tell you. Do I miss having a congregation that I can stand before every Sunday morning and help nurture during the week? Of course.

But as I reflect on those years, I'm positive of one thing: There's no way I could have done that work without the anointing of the Holy Spirit, without the power of God in my life, without the love of Christ nudging me to keep on going, and without my family standing willingly by my side.

That's what I want you to hear, pastor. Whatever stage you're in, make the most of it. Don't regret it. Don't find fault with it. Don't be obsessed with going to another stage. See what God can do for you where you are. Let Him use your gifts and graces to His glory.

I'll guarantee you one thing—some day, some place, you'll look back down your long trail of service and say, "Thank God! Thank God He gave me courage. Thank God He gave me patience. Thank God I didn't quit. Thank God for a place of ministry."

Not only is our God the God of the mountaintops, but He's also the God of the valleys, and He loves you just the same either place. Best of all, He will never leave you or forsake you.

The week I completed this book, I had occasion to address a group of pastors in the Midwest. At the end of my time with them, they presented me with a plaque entitled "Ministry." It quoted 1 Timothy 1:12: "I thank Christ Jesus our Lord, who hath enabled me, for that he counted me faithful, putting me into the ministry."

In a few words, the apostle Paul echoed my thoughts! I trust they are yours as well. Stay the course, my friend!

About the Contributors

H. B. London Jr. is vice president of ministry outreach/pastoral ministries for Focus on the Family in Colorado Springs, Colorado, and a former pastor. He is affectionately known as a "pastor to pastors."

Archibald Hart is dean and professor of psychology of the Graduate School of Psychology, Fuller Theological Seminary, in Pasadena, California.

Gordon MacDonald is the senior pastor of Grace Chapel in Lexington, Massachusetts.

Jerry Bridges is a popular teacher and speaker who served for many years with The Navigators.

John Trent is the president of Encouraging Words in Phoenix, Arizona, and a former pastor.

Dennis Rainey is executive director of FamilyLife Ministries in Little Rock, Arkansas.

Eugene H. Peterson is professor of spiritual theology at Regent College in Vancouver, British Columbia, and a former pastor.

Bobb Biehl is the founder and president of Master Planning Group International in Lake Mary, Florida.

Kent Hughes is the senior pastor of College Church in Wheaton, Illinois.

George Barna is the president of Barna Research Group in Oxnard, California, and a former pastor.

John Maxwell is the founder of INJOY ministries in San Diego, California, and a former pastor.

Os Guinness is a writer and speaker and the Senior Fellow of the Trinity Forum in northern Virginia.

Donald Bubna is a pastor-at-large for the Christian and Missionary Alliance in Salem, Oregon.

Francis Schaeffer (1912-1984) was a prolific author, founder of L'Abri Fellowship, and a former pastor.

Other Great Resources for the Pastor and His Ministry

Let's face it. As a pastor, you're busy—period. And keeping that kind of pace is tiring. Rejuvenate with Focus on the Family's "Pastor to Pastor" resources.

"Pastor to Pastor" Newsletter and Audio Cassette Series

Designed specifically to meet the needs of your hectic lifestyle, the *Pastor to Pastor audio cassette series* features uplifting interviews with leading pastors and speakers on topics that will help you handle challenges both behind and beyond the pulpit. Hosted by H. B. London Jr., each bimonthly two-cassette package offers in-depth insight from a biblical point of view.

Accompanying the steady stream of support on cassette comes the *Pastor to Pastor newsletter.* It's packed with encouragement and relevant information that will lift you up as a person *and* a minister. You'll find answers to the difficult questions about balancing time and finances, living a healthy lifestyle, overcoming sexual temptation, recovering from infidelity, preparing for revival, resolving conflict in the church, and many other concerns unique to the pastorate—all in a refreshingly honest manner.

"The Pastor's Weekly Briefing" Newsletter

And for church leaders who want accurate, up-to-the-minute information on current events, *The Pastor's Weekly Briefing* can be faxed to your office or home each Thursday evening. Designed for your convenience, this insightful newsletter will keep you abreast of the latest issues that affect you, your family, and the members of your congregation.

Pastor's Family Magazine

As a pastor, you're the one many people turn to for guidance, help, and counsel. Yet, you and your family need support and understanding just as much as the next person. So Focus on the Family created *Pastor's Family,* a new bimonthly magazine with 32 encouraging pages addressing such important topics as spending time with your children, rekindling romance in your marriage, finding real friends, being a pastor's wife in the '90s, and much more—all in an easy-to-read format the entire family will enjoy.

For more information about any of these insightful resources, write:

Focus on the Family
Colorado Springs, CO 80995
1-800-A-FAMILY (1-800-232-6459) or (719) 531-3400

In Canada, write:

Focus on the Family
P.O. Box 9800, Stn. Terminal
Vancouver, B.C. V6B 4G3
1-800-661-9800 or (604) 684-8333

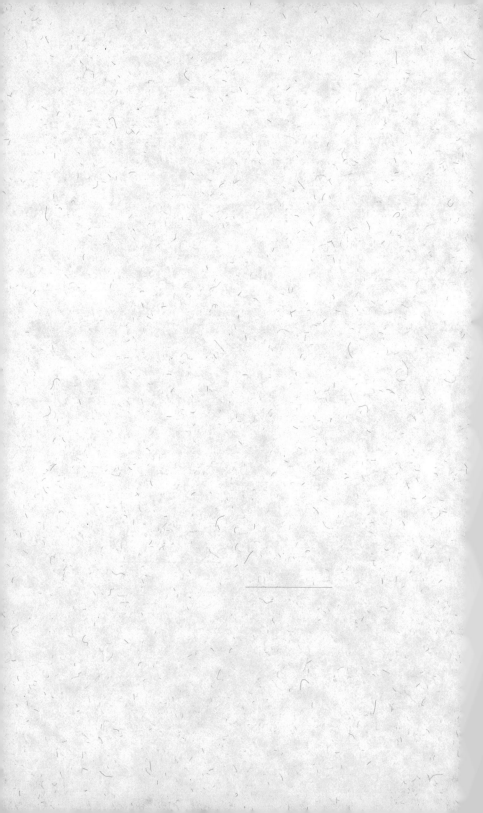